LOVING YOURSELF UNCONDITIONALLY

A Book of total love, acceptance and reassurance, wherever your journey is now

Valerie Barnes is a Therapist, Healer, Teacher and Visionary. She lectures on Life and Living. Valerie lives a simple, authentic and uncomplicated life in the Gentle Way – the Way of the Heart – which is unlimited and effortless.

She devotes her life to healing, teaching meditation and helping others to find their own path within themselves. Valerie also helps in schools teaching children to listen to their hearts, create their own life and find happiness in themselves, regardless of what is happening in their outer world.

-o-0-o-

LOVING YOURSELF UNCONDITIONALLY

A Book of total love, acceptance and reassurance, wherever your journey is now

Valerie Barnes

LOVING YOURSELF
UNCONDITIONALLY

A Book of total love, acceptance
and reassurance, wherever your
journey is now

Olympia Publishers
London

www.olympiapublishers.com
OLYMPIA PAPERBACK EDITION

Copyright © Valerie Barnes 2010

The right of Valerie Barnes to be identified as author of
this work has been asserted in accordance with sections 77 and 78 of
the Copyright, Designs and Patents Act 1988.

All Rights Reserved

No reproduction, copy or transmission of this publication
may be made without written permission.
No paragraph of this publication may be reproduced,
copied or transmitted save with the written permission of the publisher,
or in accordance with the provisions
of the Copyright Act 1956 (as amended).

Any person who commits any unauthorised act in relation to
this publication may be liable to criminal
prosecution and civil claims for damage.

A CIP catalogue record for this title is
available from the British Library.

ISBN: 978-1-84897-053-3

First Published in 2010

Olympia Publishers
60 Cannon Street
London
EC4N 6NP

Printed in Great Britain

Acknowledgements

I would like to say a huge Thank You to my sister, Elaine, for all her loving help. To my illustrator and friend, Amanda, for her exquisite gift. To my friend, Claire, for sourcing out such a helpful publisher.

Special Love and blessings to all my family, especially my daughter, Tania, my two sons Ian and Paul. Thank you for all they have taught me and for giving me five grandchildren and one great granddaughter, with their partners.

Special love to my friends, Christine and Barry, who are always there for me.

Thank you to Mark and Penny.

I am truly grateful to all who have accompanied me on my journey back to Heaven – they all know who they are – too many to mention.

I thank God for the miracle that we all are.

Contents

HOW TO USE THIS BOOK 19

THE KEY TO LIFE 20

IT IS THE THOUGHTS YOU THINK THAT CAUSE THE EMOTIONS 33

FEAR OF GETTING IT WRONG 35

WHAT IS THE AUTHENTIC SELF 38

LOVING YOUR SELF AS YOU ARE LOVED 39

WHAT IS HEALING? 40

WHAT IS STRESS? 41

SIN 43

I DON'T WANT TO BE A LEADER 46

THE PATH 47

YOUR WAY IS PERFECT 48

FEELINGS AND THE HEART 49

TRUST ME 50

WHAT'S IT LIKE LIVING IN HEAVEN ON EARTH 51

SADNESS 52

FRESH START 53

TELLING OFF 54

LETTER FROM MY ANGELS 55

LOVE AND ACCEPTANCE	55
MY ANGELS	56
THE KEY	56
ALONENESS	58
EXCUSES	60
LONELY	62
ANGER	63
ANGER (2)	64
PRIDE	65
BITTER FEELINGS	66
BITTERNESS AND RESENTMENT	67
WHEN WILL THE BITTERNESS END?	68
DEPLETION	69
REVENGE	70
THE SPIDER'S WEB	72
THE GAME'S OVER	74
I JUST WANT SOMEONE TO MAKE IT BETTER	75
TIRED OF IT ALL	76
IT'S GETTING ON MY NERVES	78
LIFELESS FEELINGS	79
STOP THE BLAMING!	80

IT'S NOT MY FAULT	81
I REMEMBER	82
THE FAMILY TREE	83
SOFTNESS	84
CHOICE	85
COMPASSION	86
CONFUSION	87
COURAGE AND STRENGTH	88
TO BE OR NOT TO BE	89
THE WOW – THE WORLD OF WONDER	91
CREATION	92
CREATING AND CREATION	93
COMMITMENT TO SELF	93
DENIAL…	95
PROCESS (1)	97
DEPRESSION	98
IT'S NEVER ENOUGH – DISSATISFIED	100
LETTER TO ME FROM GOD WITHIN:	101
GUILT	102
TENDERNESS – TO MY FRIEND	103
I AM FREE!	105

GRACE	106
THANK YOU GOD	107
HUMILITY	108
RESISTANCE	109
IRRITATIONS (DIVINE INTERRUPTIONS) TO LISTEN	112
LETTING GO INTO JOY	114
LIMBO	115
WHAT A RELIEF	116
THE OLD WAYS HANG ON – BUT THE RIVER MUST FLOW	117
LET DOWN	118
FREEDOM?	120
YOU ARE ENOUGH	122
LET'S BEGIN AGAIN	124
SLEEPLESSNESS	125
THE OPPOSITE OF TRUST – ANXIETY AND WORRY	126
DRIFTING AIMLESSLY – I FEEL LIKE A ROBOT WITH THE WORKINGS REMOVED	127
LETTING GO	129
REJECTION	132
LETTING GO	134
BE STILL	135

FROM WORRY TO CARE FREENESS	136
WHAT IS LOVE – LOVE IS TIME	137
NO MORE PAIN! THE END OF GRIEF	138
PAIN	139
WHAT YOUR LOVE MEANS TO ME	141
PEACE	142
PERFECTION	144
POVERTY CONSCIOUSNESS	146
POWER	148
PROCESS (2)	149
LETTING OFF STEAM AND BEING ME	151
THE PRESSURE COOKER – TIME AND ENERGY	152
QUESTIONS TO ASK WITHIN YOURSELF	153
SATISFACTION	154
OVERWHELMED	157
THE CHOICE IS YOURS	158
THE SIMPLE PLEASURES IN LIFE FOR ME ARE –	159
SWEET SORROW	160
BE STILL AND LISTEN TO THE CALL OF THE SOUL	161
GAZING AND DREAMING – AN EXTENSION OF TIME	163
STAYING STRONG	164

WHO AM I? 165

EYES WIDE OPEN 167

A COLD MARCH DAY – HOME IS WHERE MY HEART IS 168

NOBODY HEARS ME.. 170

THE POWER OF LOVE AND FORGIVENESS..................... 171

THE BIG LIE – THE ILLUSION 173

OPPOSITES 174

THROUGH THE EYES OF A CHILD 175

A LETTER TO MY 'SELF' FROM 'MY' HOLY SPIRIT........... 176

WHERE AM "I" NOW?.. 177

MY LIFE 178

WAKE-UP! WAKE-UP! 179

STANDING STRAIGHT AND TALL, LIKE THE OLD OAK TREE............ 180

THIS IS A MESSAGE FROM MICHAEL THE GREAT.......... 181

BLISS 183

MY DEAREST ONE 184

TO BE AN ANGEL 185

WHAT I SEE CLEARLY NOW 186

WHAT NOW?... 189

LOVE YOUR CHILDREN FOR WHO THEY ARE 191

NOT WHAT THEY DO.. 191

A MOTHER'S WORDS FOR MY SONS AND DAUGHTER 192

MY TRIBUTE TO MUM 193

WHO AM I? (2) 195

WHY DO WE DO TOO MUCH 196

THIS IS THE PRICE WE PAY FOR SUCCESS 197

TRY TO REMEMBER 199

STUCK IN THE MUD 200

HEART ATTACK! 201

"SURVIVAL OF A HEART ATTACK" 203

GOD'S COMMANDMENTS TO ME 205

FREEDOM AND JOY 206

HOME AT LAST 207

TAKING CONTROL AGAIN 208

MY IDEA OF HEAVEN ON EARTH 209

DOORS WITHIN 210

How To Use This Book

These pages contain my feelings, emotions, thoughts, observations and conversations with God on my journey back home to Heaven within myself.

Heaven is a state of mind aligned with a feeling of absolute love, peace and stillness in the heart that never goes away, regardless of what is happening around you in the outer world.

I suggest sitting quietly with the book and, after reading the introduction, letting it open at a particular page and reading only as much as you need.

Or… asking the question of your heart which page you need and then read that section.

This book carries my essence, loving you and accepting you with all your thoughts and feelings on your earth journey.

Why wait until you die to experience perfection and Heaven for yourself?

-o-o-0-o-o-

There may be some parts of the book that do not make sense at the time of reading. If so, move on to something that does.

As you go through your own layers of consciousness to your deeper layers, your perspective changes completely so things make more sense to you.

The world reflects back to you all your deepest thoughts and feelings, opinions and beliefs until you can love and accept yourself unconditionally.

THE KEY TO LIFE

This book is written with one purpose in mind and that is to show people how to find for themselves the KEY TO LIFE AND LIVING HERE ON EARTH.

I believe we are all first and foremost Spiritual Beings in essence and are here to learn HOW TO BE human with all the feelings, emotions, challenges, pain and sadness – until we have learned how to love ourselves as we are loved by God with NO CONDITIONS AT ALL.

THIS IS UNCONDITIONAL LOVE.

When we can love ourselves as we are right now, we get to co-create with God our own world as we want it to be HEAVEN ON EARTH OR PARADISE.

This journey may take many lifetimes, but many on Earth at this time are ready to wake up to who and what we are and why we are here. Many of us will find HEAVEN ON EARTH AND ABSOLUTE PEACE.

Heaven is an experience within ourselves, a state of mind and a feeling in the heart of being one with God and the whole universe. When you experience this within yourself your own outer world becomes a living reality as heaven for future generations to experience.

MY LIFE IS NOW FULL OF REAL (NOT ILLUSIONARY) MAGIC AND MIRACLES, BEAUTY AND LOVE.

<u>WEIGHT</u>   What is it really about
           it is <u>not</u> about food!
           But <u>BEING THE GREATER SELF</u>

<u>HEAVINESS</u> Why are we growing bigger in order to see the reflection of our 'Greater' self.

What is the weight this world is carrying
Trying to free itself of the past,
The wars, the bitterness, the battle within
Each human being longing to be
Free to express themselves
To be themselves
Without fear of judgment of others
Free to be different as we are meant to be
Alive and happy to be here on earth
As the old Web is untangled and the Hurt is revealed then the misunderstandings can reveal the Truth – that we are not alone but we are all <u>one</u> and if one Human Being is hurting still then, that affects us all, for the energy, the vibration is felt through that silent communication of the Web that has been spun by us all.

As the Butterfly flaps its wings the vibrations can be felt the world over – so imagine all we carry in our hearts individually and multiply it – this will help you understand why the world is depleted and needs us all to heal our hearts on an individual level. It's the only way to create a new world for the coming generations.

If everyone looked into their hearts and did their own inner journey imagine how powerful we would all become:
           One Heart
           One Soul
           One Mind

Beating in Love.

When your heart is healed you can never harm yourself or anyone else ever again!

No more outward battles
No more family feuds
No more pain
No more sacrifice

Just Love and Peace/Joy for all.

BELIEVE and it can be so

For your Belief
Becomes your Reality.

This is the Best way to make a difference to the world energy. Imagine the Love Vibrations from yourself when you have healed. They will communicate your Love to the whole world. When you are in touch with your own Purity all you receive is Love.

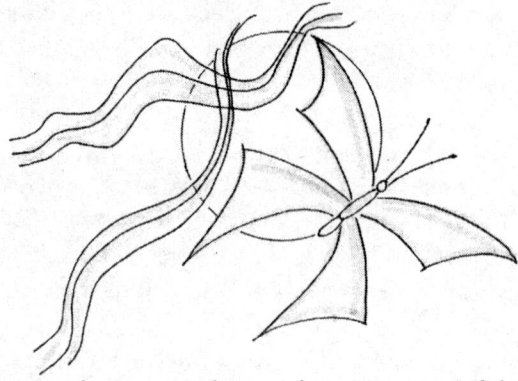

This journey took me several years, but every step of the way was worth it for HOW I FEEL AND FUNCTION TODAY AS THE GREATER ME!

-o-o-0-o-o-

Let me share my journey with you, take my hand and walk with me to find your own path within yourself.

When I was a child and all through my life I knew I could separate myself from reality and be in my own world when times were hard and I struggled with life's challenges as a child, a girl, a wife, a business partner and mother of three. Deep inside me I always knew I had immense strength to overcome whatever life threw at me. I trusted MYSELF, although I didn't realise it at the time.

My book is not about my outer journey in the world, but a much more exciting and interesting inner journey into the unknown. I journeyed into the deep unconscious mind (the mind of the whole world wherein lie all the things that scare us, but also the treasures and abundance of life). The opposites of the coin, the Dark and the Light.

Sometimes this is called the dark night of the soul and yes it takes a lot of Courage, Patience and Faith to make this journey but, when you get to the Light at the end, there's nothing to experience but the Purest and Deepest and most exquisite Love and the Fear loses all its Power over you for good.

I have shared my journey with many Light Travellers, who have each and every one contributed to my own healing and self recognition and I thank them all – too many to mention – but they know who they are, for we are of one heart and mind and body and they still accompany me and I them.

When travelling through the darkness my energy felt heavy and weighed me down, but the light would always lift me out again with a taste of what was to come.

The emotions such as…

- Anger
- Hate
- Sadness
- Shame
- Resentment
- Bitterness
- Blame
- Jealousy

…are what I term as <u>heavy feelings</u> rather than the word negative, which implies that they are wrong, so we <u>feel wrong</u> for feeling them. They sit heavy in the heart, so make us feel heavy, tired and lethargic, whereas the lighter emotions of peace, love, joy, contentment and bliss are light in the heart and the body, making us happy and carefree.

Alternating between these feelings and emotions can be like a roller coaster ride, but what I have learned along my long and difficult journey at times are the short cuts, which I shall call short cuts to God within ME. You only learn short cuts by doing lots of things the long way first until you find there is ONLY ONE WAY LEFT! The Easy Way with least effort involved.

This book is intended to help you understand your life and your purpose on Earth. It's very simple and easy if you follow <u>Your Rules</u> in your heart not your head any more. For your heart is connected to the source of it all, the 'Oneness', and in order to give and receive all your heart desires you need harmony and balance first of all.

The way to achieve this is by going within yourself – (see page 209 on opening doors within) – and listening to that kind loving voice (Call it God, call it source – Soul –universe, or just your Higher Power – it doesn't matter) but you will <u>know,</u> for it never gives you any messages of Fear or limits you being your Authentic self. Listen to the 'Voice'. The Real Truth is always wonderful whatever <u>you</u> may think of yourself.

Sit quietly and ask your Heart to tell you the Truth (the <u>real</u> Truth – not your Truth) for that can be distorted by your emotions, experiences, beliefs, culture and by Fear of not being good enough or worthy enough. These are just the labels of Society and just because they come from Authority figures (people we expect to KNOW) don't forget their Truth could be distorted too, based on their beliefs and experiences and also motivation for Power and Control. Live <u>'your'</u> life only, not someone else's, otherwise what really is the point if each generation only does the same, believes the same and acts the same as the last one – there's no sense in that, is there? Question all you believe and ask: "is this True for me, does it work, make me happy, feel alive?" And discard it if it doesn't'. Change your mind. It's Your Mind – Your Future – Your Choice.

Don't store thoughts that do not serve you for all you do is re-create more of the same life you have been living. This is very easy to do when you know how – if you find a thought or belief keeps coming into your head, <u>ask your Loving voice</u> to just remove this Seed of Doubt and Fear from your Consciousness and move on to the next thought. Don't work at it, think about it or worry about it, just let go and it will be deleted.

A good way to think of it, in this computer age we live in, is to press the delete button when your trash can is full. If you are holding on to old thoughts and beliefs and not downloading every day, then you will be on overload and feel clogged and heavy hearted. In order to live in today, and The Now, the screen of your consciousness needs to be clear to constantly take in new information and deal with what life is presenting you with today without interference from the past or future thoughts.
This keeps your energy focused all the time in the NOW. You wouldn't pull up on the screen everything at once in your computer

(brain), past present future (fear) would you, for you would not be able to focus or have clarity now. This is what you do all the time – so your life never changes. Your brain automatically sorts out what you <u>need</u> to remember if you trust this and not keep telling yourself you can't remember. If you don't remember it's because you don't need to, it's not that important (only your Fear voice telling you so). Why would you need all that TRIVIA anyway – what I ate or did yesterday is of no consequence to me NOW.

Your subconscious mind (all thoughts, feelings and beliefs from childhood) does not distinguish between what is Real and what is False. It takes what you think and say very literally. So, if you tell yourself anything negative often enough your messages are passed to the body and the body acts it out. For example "I am useless at D.I.Y." automatically blocks the brain from thinking it through and the body from following it through and taking the <u>ACTION TO PRODUCE OR CREATE</u>. "I AM USELESS" becomes your outer reality but not the REAL TRUTH.

When we have a thought "let's go on holiday" … or plan to build a house, we then look at the choices based on several things

What we think we can afford
Where we want to go
When we want to go etc

We think the thoughts of what we want and our brain and body take action on the thoughts and follow through (this is Creation). Thought becomes the word, the word becomes the deed. We are the Creator of our own thoughts and the feelings are created by our thoughts and reactions (perception) to what is happening around us. Emotions are thoughts in action flowing through the body and we act them out. If we attach a label to ourselves such as:

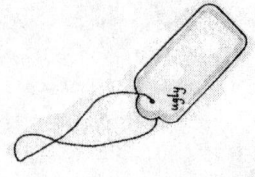
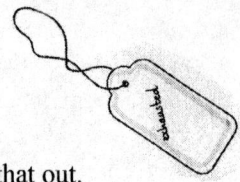

I am a pessimist – then we act that out.
I am a poor loser – then we act that out.
I am no good at sports – then we act that out.
I am stupid – and then we act that out.

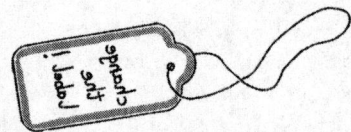
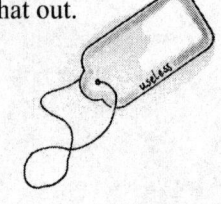

What are you telling yourself every day? Most of the thoughts we think on a daily basis are the same so we keep on creating the same thing and nothing changes! If we believe we are not good enough then we act as if we are not by limiting what we allow ourselves to have in life. It is really very simple. Our <u>Belief is our Reality</u>.

We act out a role according to our thoughts and beliefs about ourselves, but some of these are not <u>real truth</u>, we have <u>chosen</u> to believe them so that we can HIDE the real "authentic self" we came to be. It seems easier to hide and play small, than stand out in a crowd, but in actual fact it is hard work playing small!

Why do we want to hide, you may well ask. It scares us – "our greatness" is more fearful than our "smallness." The Greater Self has no fear and <u>trusts</u> life to give us all we need, when we need it. Our smaller self lives in fear of never having our needs met and always searching in the world for <u>someone</u> or <u>something</u> to meet our needs. The reason we are so scared of "BEING GREAT" is that we will stand out in the crowd with our uniqueness and we would rather blend in with everyone else and be like them. We are all born to be leaders and great people, but take on the labels, opinions, beliefs and even the diagnosis of what is WRONG with us rather than asking within ourselves: "IS THIS RIGHT FOR ME?" "DO I CHOOSE TO BELIEVE THIS TO BE <u>ABSOLUTE TRUTH FOR ME?"</u>

The Absolute Truth has been so distorted by what we believe to be True. We are not worthless, poor, inhibited beings if we <u>do not</u> make the choice to be.

We are awesome, fantastic, wonderful, marvellous BEINGS of light and love if we choose to REMEMBER WHO WE ARE AND OUR PURPOSE FOR "BEING" HERE. Notice I keep underlining and emphasising the word "<u>BEING</u>". We are not "DOINGS" we are human beings and our purpose in life is not what we do but who we are being and the gift we are here to give is our uniqueness and special way of giving our love – these gifts are some of what we all come into this world with in our "Hearts"

LOVE
INSPIRATION
COMPASSION
STRENGTH
TENDERNESS
UNDERSTANDING
KINDNESS
HEALING
LISTENING SKILLS
SPEAKING SKILLS

These are the gifts of Being – we do not have to do our Purpose in Life but purely be it. <u>The Innocent Child</u>. Yes, we choose everything that happens to us on some level either conscious or unconscious together with other souls who journey with us in Life. Co-creation. Indeed this is a remarkable journey we choose to undertake to understand at the deepest possible level what Real Unconditional Love is about.

It is not about neediness, dependency, or inadequacy, if it hurts it is NOT LOVE. There is NO PAIN with God's Love, only Joy and Bliss and our journey on Earth is to find this. It will never be found by expecting someone else to give it to you, by having a partner, children, friends, a good job, a brilliant home or lots of money. All these will be wonderful and valued highly, but not needed for happiness. Happiness, true happiness, is only to be found within the self, love for the self and your greatness is the only way to go, for how can you give what you don't have.

If you don't have a Full Self and Self Love then you cannot give it. When you find this within you it flows from you with no effort involved and flows back to you with no effort. This is our True Nature – it has no choice but to return, it is such a Powerful Energy and No Fear can touch it or change it!

If you are not getting what you want and need in the outside world then you have to go within yourself to find it and stop looking outside yourself. The easiest way to do this is to sit quietly with yourself and ask – everyone knows they have within themselves a Higher Power, Wise Self (Authority Voice) call it God, Divine Intelligence, Creator, Buddha, the name does not matter, but once you hand your problems, relationships, life and other people over to that Power, it is done through you not BY YOU with the least effort and for the good of all. If you try to 'DO' it on your own it is hard work and struggle and sacrifice and, let's face it my friend, you would not be reading this if your way was working out and giving you what you need and want!

When it is sorted through you not by you it sets your Energy free to enjoy the things life brings you including the Challenges. You rise to each one knowing your Higher Power knows best and will guide you through anything. You learn to Trust in yourself, your own Authority and your own Power.

So when do we choose not to shine this Light/Love without worrying what others may think of us. The answer to that is when we feel someone has hurt us emotionally or physically, <u>always always</u> when we <u>are young</u>, so the pattern for life is set with our thoughts and beliefs we take on. In my many experiences of healing adults, this is usually between the ages of 2 – 6 years old.

When we have been hurt either physically or emotionally we have to BLAME SOMEONE OR SOMETHING – this straightaway makes us power<u>less</u> to change the situation. We make a CHOICE to hurt them back by not shining that light and giving them our Love – but also we hurt ourselves by not allowing the Love in and not choosing to Heal ourselves either physically or emotionally.

When we hold on to the <u>PAIN</u> instead of thinking: they have the Power to hurt me – but I have the Power to Heal that hurt or hold on to it and continue HURTING myself until I wake up to MY POWER WITHIN. This is <u>not condoning</u> any action by anyone, but it is accepting our Greatness so we can keep giving our <u>Gift of Being Our True Self</u> and receiving the same gifts back for ourselves. What we give out we receive back.

Example:
Someone has decided that after twenty years of being married with children resulting from that partnership, they want to leave the relationship because it's not working. The partner is hurt by the rejection he/she feels, blames the other one because he/she feels inadequate to cope, rejects their own self, then wants to hit back with hurting their partner rather than healing the hurt in their own heart and moving on. They <u>hold</u> on to the hurting and punishing themselves and each other, which keeps them from giving their authentic loving self to the children and the rest of the family.

Then the guilt sets in – Guilt = self-punishment imprisonment (locked up love). Self-punishment – giving ourselves pain by withholding our love and not allowing ourselves to receive it either. The Heart Centre is like a two-way valve. If you are not letting the love flow out it cannot flow back in (hence heart attacks) when our heart hits back and stops the blood (life force energy) from giving us life

- The Ultimate Self Punishment!

We think far too much and analyse far too much, wasting time and energy on making ourselves wrong for what we are thinking and feeling. Every time we make ourselves wrong we hurt inside in some way.

Think of a time when you have been so hurt and angry with what someone has said or done, then afterwards felt guilty and cut your finger on a knife – burnt your hand or stubbed your toe or, even worse, had a bad accident. Work it out back to your thoughts about YOU AND YOUR BEHAVIOUR. IT IS ALWAYS ABOUT SELF.

We are taught that we are <u>good</u> if we are <u>doing</u> what we're told, conforming to other people's ideas of right and wrong, instead of being told <u>we are always</u> good inside, it is our behaviour that is not always good. Children learn from what we do more than what we say. They want to feel loved and Special. That is all anyone wants.

Love = TIME AND RESPECT FOR EACH OTHER.

Give someone these two things and they will respond lovingly in the end. Love is the Ultimate Power we have in our hearts. Love can heal emotionally and physically setting us free to live again and face the challenges our Soul chooses for us.

-o-o-0-o-o-

It is the Thoughts you think that cause the Emotions

Until you make yourself Right with what you <u>are</u> feeling you won't <u>feel</u> happy.

You were <u>born</u> to be <u>happy</u>.

It is not the Feelings/Emotions that cause us physical symptoms, but the Making Ourselves Wrong for having them. That is where the Hardness (see Hard Hearted!) to Ourselves is coming from. It is self attack! Heart attack! We make ourselves WRONG for our so-called weakness!

It's ok and normal to feel
Resentful
Jealous
Angry
Selfish
Bitter
Anxious
Sad
Impatient
Intolerant
Afraid

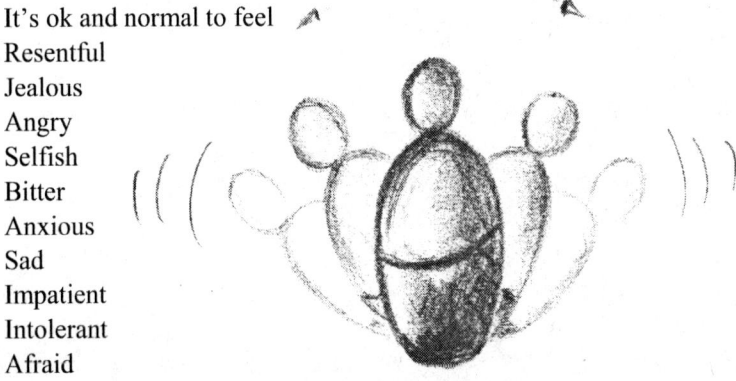

These are NOT NEGATIVE. No Emotion is negative. Negative means wrong. Feeling wrong hurts us.

It's ok to want and desire. It's not unspiritual it's REAL and we are here to be <u>REAL</u> and Authentic.

These feelings are <u>not negative</u> they are Human and experienced from childhood onwards, but we are made to <u>feel</u> guilty and wrong for these and the wrong feeling attached to them makes us heavy and weighed down (heavy energy) not light and free.

Love your ANGER, RESENTMENT, JEALOUSY for what it is showing you, but do <u>not</u> project it on to others. Own it as yours. <u>THIS WILL EMPOWER YOU, NOT MAKE YOU POWERLESS.</u>

These feelings are just to guide us through life so we can stay balanced and poised. If we are feeling jealous, then we learn why, accept the feeling for what it is showing us, and restore our balance again.

To Master our Emotions – does not mean we don't need to feel them, it means to accept them at all times – it is ok to feel them. We then move through them as do small children gracefully without being knocked off balance for long.

<u>GUILT</u>
There is no guilt if you do not make yourself wrong for what you are feeling and thinking, so there is no need for self punishment. Without self punishment you do not <u>HURT</u> inside, so do not project any <u>HURT</u> or <u>PAIN</u> onto others.

The reality is what you are thinking and Feeling is there – why deny it, it's being dishonest with yourself and others. Accept the thoughts and feelings and they lose their <u>Power over You</u>! Deny them and they will haunt you for life. They are meant to be so!

Think about it every time you make yourself wrong for being Angry (this is passed down to the children <u>that they are WRONG</u>) you are Denying yourself the opportunity your Soul has chosen for you to learn what works and doesn't work in your life.

We learn by our mistakes – they are the Mechanism by which we learn what works for us. If we resist the lesson it just keeps showing up larger and larger until we have no CHOICE. Imagine how much easier it would be if we accepted each lesson as it came along and moved through it easily without FEAR.

FEAR OF GETTING IT WRONG

This Fear is the only thing that holds us back from exploring our Full Potential.

If we accepted in our Mind totally it's ok to get it wrong (because there is really no wrong – only exploring and experiencing) we would do so much more in life, and achieve so much more for ourselves.

Guilt causes us to sabotage our own good by telling us we are never good enough. We are never enough as we are.
We are not worthy
So we over compensate for this by

>Doing too much to prove ourselves
>Giving to others before ourselves
>Being too nice for our <u>own</u> good builds up resentment inside.

It keeps us locked in our own prison walls. No-one does it to us, we do it to ourselves. No-one punishes us – we do a good enough job of it ourselves. No-one judges us – we do it to ourselves.

All of this stops us from allowing in the Love, because we don't feel Worthy of that Love. How <u>could we</u> if we feel <u>so sinful</u>?

All God gives us is Unconditional Love – that means <u>NO CONDITIONS AT ALL</u>.

All we have to do is Allow it in, but we <u>will not</u> allow it in if we are always feeling we are guilty and sinful.

We <u>learn</u> by doing things that don't work and make us happy, so we have to have an opposite for everything

Love	Hate
Black	White
Pain	Comfort
Ease	Dis-ease
Wrong	Right

If you are comfortable with <u>all</u> your feelings, then your body will be comfortable. If you hurt yourself with your thinking, then you will <u>feel pain</u> in your body or discomfort which, over a period of time, becomes illness and dis-ease – it is that simple.

Your body manifests what is inside sometimes over generations of families, so if you are not listening to your Body Messages, then you are disconnected from God and Life as it should be.

Your Body gives you feedback all the time until you can Master your emotions and feelings from within.

If you are not Living Within Yourself then you are going without and there's <u>NEVER ENOUGH</u>

- Love
- Time
- Peace
- Joy
- Money
- Nourishment
- Abundance

It's all within you – start searching – don't wait!

I have experienced many, many things in my life that do not work for me and make me happy but, in that process of elimination, there is only <u>one</u> thing left and that is…

When I don't make myself wrong and hurt myself then I feel happy and comfortable to be ME and I love and accept myself as I am right now. Bring on more learning experiences, now I know how to handle them with Grace and Ease!

Thank you to all my Angels, my Earth Angels, my Ascended Masters and of course to God for giving me the opportunity to share my life with you.

Special thanks to my family who have given me the Best Lessons in Life.

And my Soul Mates Ken (my husband) and Christine. We are all one and the same. We are the Source of it all.

To all my fellow brothers and sisters whose books and tapes I've shared along the way, far too many to mention, but they will know.

-o-o-0-o-o-

What is the Authentic Self

It's the Self you came to be
Full of self confidence, self worth and self esteem.
It is the Greater Self in all its Glory not tainted by any aspects of the outside world, not affected by world opinions, beliefs or even laws.
It is the Self that knows all and believes and Trusts totally in their own judgment and own authority. It is a Self who cannot be harmed, hurt, or affected by what is happening in the world.
Being in the World, but not of the world.

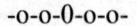

-o-o-0-o-o-

LOVING YOUR SELF AS YOU ARE LOVED

How do we know we are loved? (Deserving implies we have to earn it!! <u>NOT TRUE</u>). When we are ready to listen to our heart.

When we are born we don't have a label attached to us,
But everything we need to know is inside us and
We start to remember when our PLAN for our LIFE
Is not working out or making us happy.

Knowing and believing are different.
What we believe is not always the real truth.
What your heart knows comes from your Soul
And has a voice.

This voice tells no fear, no judgment, no wrong or right, no bad or good
Just love and acceptance of all you are.

DO YOU WANT YOUR EARTH JOURNEY TO BE A HAPPY OR UNHAPPY JOURNEY – HEAVEN OR HELL?

DO YOU WANT TO BE A LIGHT IN THE WORLD OR A SHADOW?

START LISTENING WITHIN.

-o-o-0-o-o-

What is Healing?

Healing is making whole from the inside. When you feel whole, you feel part of the oneness with other human beings, you see the Light in everyone (though more in some than others)

It is also about healing the world, by healing yourself first, then giving that gift to others in your community. You feel more connected to the whole and secure within yourself. When one person raises his or her consciousness (awareness) then you assist everyone around you to raise his or hers.

Healing helps you to feel good about yourself and increases strength and support within yourself.

What is a Healer?

A Healer is a person who already sees the Light (goodness) in others and is willing to share their time and their love in order to improve the brightness in that light by healing the dark emotions and feelings which cover up that light and prevent the receiver from giving their true selves to their family, friends and the world.

It is not about curing, because there is nothing to cure in the spirit or soul, only lessons to learn. We get stuck in the physical reality so that we cannot see the bigger picture of who we really are.

The Light (Love) will overcome the darkness, which is really fear (Ego) and this will disappear when people work together as a whole and not just for themselves and their own needs.

As a result of healing the emotions and feelings held in the heart, physical problems often just disappear and the people feel lighter and freer to be themselves.

-o-o-0-o-o-

WHAT IS STRESS?

This has become a MIND "VIRUS" that is spreading so quickly amongst society that even our children have caught it. IT CAUSES ILL HEALTH!

STRESS is a label we wear that says to the world
"I AM NOT COPING WITH MY LIFE"

in other words

"I AM INADEQUATE!"

THIS IS A LIE (AN ILLUSION)

We come into this life with NO FEAR and fully equipped with all we need for our life, but have forgotten where to look. The answers are all in the HEART not the head. We need to wake up and step out of our conditioning and conditioned responses – this is all fear we have been taught.

WE CAN LIVE FEARLESSLY – I DID NOT YEARS AGO, BUT I DO NOW AND IT IS POSSIBLE FOR US ALL.

When you say you are Stressed this vibrational energy goes out into the world sending a message of WEAK! WEAK! WEAK!

THIS IS NOT TRUE – YOU ARE STRONG AND POWERFUL BEYOND MEASURE.

Also our bodies register this feeling and we feel weak and tired (children too). Our muscles and cells respond to our thinking.

DON'T THINK IT, DON'T BELIEVE IT, OR IT WILL BECOME YOUR REALITY – WHAT YOU THINK ABOUT EXPANDS.

START THINKING I AM CALM AND PEACEFUL – GO WITHIN YOUR HEART AND ASK FOR HELP AND LISTEN. YOU WILL THEN CREATE MORE OF THAT REALITY.

WHAT YOU PUT AFTER THE WORDS "I AM …" BECOMES YOUR NEW REALITY AND BELIEF.

-o-o-0-o-o-

SIN

What is sin?

It is what we create in our own minds, we need to learn to love and forgive ourselves and each other.

There is no sin only love and peace.

I am not at all condoning peoples actions towards one another. These actions are, however, based on what people feel inside and deny, so they hurt and feel attacked, so attack back because they <u>feel</u> they are defending themselves.

When you don't attack yourself you do not attack others.

When you have an 'inner battle' going on, then it will be projected on to others for you to see what is inside yourself.

Stop fighting yourself – your Ultimate Power is defencelessness – not giving anyone an enemy to fight, for when you stop hurting yourself no-one can hurt you anymore, because you have the Power to Heal emotionally and Physically Within You. This again is God's Power, there for all.

THE ONLY SIN WE COMMIT IS WHAT WE DO TO OURSELVES AND IN SEPARATING OURSELVES FROM GOD.

When I love every little bit about myself even my non-acceptance I stop resisting Life. When I STOP RESISTING life I am in the Flow. When I'm in the Flow I'm in JOY. When I'm in Joy I am Innocent and free to be Me as I AM.

I love all my feelings and my judgment
I love my Pain

I love myself when I can't get it right
I love it when I'm Hiding Myself away, because I'm so clever (or so I think)
I love it when I feel as if I've slipped back
I love it when I'm confused
I love it when I just can't sort it out
I love it when it HURTS, it shows me I'm still alive
Love is all there is and no reasons or why's or wherefores, no justifying myself

I love it when I don't want to be responsible for anything or anyone.

I love it all.

I love myself when I don't want to do anything
I love myself when I talk too much
I love myself when I'm not being NICE
I love myself when I'm not being REAL
I love myself when I eat too much
I love myself when I drink too much
I love myself when I watch too much TV
I love myself when I feel out of balance
I love myself when I look awful
I love myself when my hair's a mess
I love myself when I look old
I love myself when I feel old
I love myself when I feel frumpy
I love myself when I'm tired
I love myself when I don't know what I want or want to do
I love myself when I feel I've lost the plot
I love myself when I feel NOTHINGNESS
I love myself when I feel UNFIT
I love myself when I feel UNHEALTHY
I love myself when I feel LOW IN SPIRIT
I love myself when I feel unproductive
This is INNOCENCE AND WONDER.

I LOVE MY POWER
This is "Being Real"

God tells me Man has turned his journey on Earth into Hell on Earth in his MIND. In order to find the Kingdom of Heaven within, he has to go through the Darkness of the Unconscious Mind (the Mind of the Whole World) 'til he comes through to the Light, facing all his Fears and Beliefs along the way.

Until you can love and accept all you feel, you cannot heal it and reach radical forgiveness, forgiveness at the very root of your family tree, so you can live in your own Light and your own Mind.

This is what is meant by being in the WORLD, but not OF the world's thinking, judgment and authority.

I am My Own Authority on everything, and never look to anyone or anything outside of myself for answers.

-o-o-0-o-o-

I don't want to be a Leader

I don't want to be a Leader
People following me everywhere

I just want to share with others
What I've learned and how to care

To watch them grow and expand their lives
Is all I need to see

I don't want to be anyone Special
I just want to be ME!

-o-o-0-o-o-

The Path

Walk on the Path of Love
Be true to yourselves and each other
You know the only way is the True Way
Through your eyes will come the Beauty of Life
And you will light the Path for others

-o-o-0-o-o-

YOUR WAY IS PERFECT

Your way is perfect and the right one for you
You can listen to others and be swayed
But come back to yourself and listen within
This is called BEING TRUE TO YOUR "SELF".

No-one else knows your path
No-one else knows your Soul
There is only one way and that's YOURS
So keep listening My Friend and the answers will come
When you just surrender it all.

In the stillness of Being (not rushing around)
It will all be revealed in time
Just ask for patience, endurance and courage
To be in this Moment in Time

The discomfort will ease when you accept how it is
It's resisting that makes it so hard.
You can't run away, there's nowhere to go
What you are looking for is inside of yourself.

But the treadmill of life keeps on pulling you back in
Till you make the decision to stop
Go within, deep within and step off the wheel (world)
Listen and wait, listen and wait

Your answers WILL come when your mind quietens down
And your HEART can be heard once more.

-o-o-0-o-o-

FEELINGS AND THE HEART

If you are not listening to your heart and your feelings –
Life is like being in a strange country and trying to find your way around without a road map and completely on your own. No guide or guidance – IMAGINE THAT!

This is **How** you Create your Life – How good is it?

-o-o-0-o-o-

TRUST ME

Come with me on a Journey
Take my hand, Trust in Me
We are going on a Journey to meet yourself
There is nothing to fear, I will hold you safe
Trust me I won't let you down

We are going on a journey
To a far off land
Where Angels fly free and so do we
In the depths of our minds and our hearts – we are one
Take my hand, hold it tight,

    TRUST ME

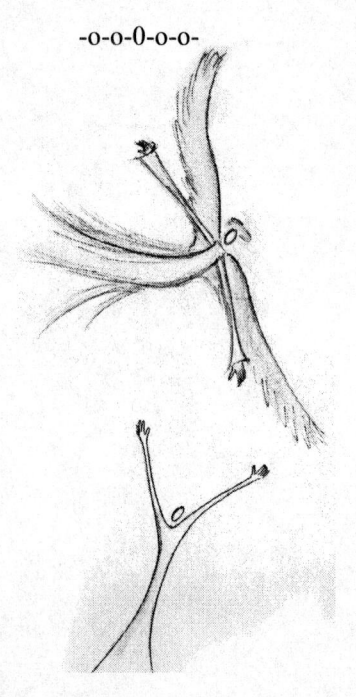

-o-o-0-o-o-

WHAT'S IT LIKE LIVING IN HEAVEN ON EARTH

You never feel alone or lonely
You have everything you need and want
You feel completely supported and protected
You never feel dissatisfied or there is not enough

TIME, LOVE, ENERGY, MONEY.

You don't feel limited
You don't feel you are responsible for anyone else (the world)
You have no pain or hurt any more
You never feel let down
You never feel wrong.

You respond only with UNCONDITIONAL LOVE AND COMPASSION
You can have whatever you want and need
Everything is taken care of for you but not by you.
Life is simple and heavenly.
Everything is perfect as it is.

Absolute freedom to be yourself, AND TO DO ONLY WHOLEHEARTEDLY WITH LOVE.

How do I know?
I KNOW BECAUSE IT'S WHERE I LIVE!

-o-o-0-o-o-

SADNESS

Sadness is the feeling you have when you have lost your True Self
(Your Spirit Self)
And your Soul seeks for you to re-unite with your heart and the
oneness with God.
Your Heart begs you to listen but you are too busy my Friend with
the stuff of life that never ends and never fulfills your needs.
Your searching outwards never works for your answers lie within
And you have to be still and quiet to hear.
God doesn't shout, but waits patiently in your heart till you are
ready to listen
And his plan for you is greater by far than any human mind can
conceive
So sit still and listen, be patient and wait
All will be revealed for those who want only the best for
themselves and their family and friends.

-o-o-0-o-o-

FRESH START

Innocence
We've set the world up this way to prove to ourselves who we are
To fully experience ourselves as One with God
It is no-one's fault
We are not to blame, we have just forgotten.

When we recognise who we are, why we are here, love and accept ourselves as we are seeing our own Innocence, then we get to create exactly what we want, when we want it.

Believe and see

Believe within and see without (or in the Reality world)

-o-o-0-o-o-

TELLING OFF

Telling off wears us down
And makes us feel small
But we do it to ourselves all day long
And our body gets tired and won't move along
Till we STOP and listen to ourselves.

Listen to your own voice
How it nags, how it judges
How it criticises everything you do
It is endless, like a record that is stuck in the groove
STOP IT, STOP IT, YOUR HEART SCREAMS TO BE RELEASED
From the onslaught of your careless thoughts.

Do you not See what you are doing to your Sacred Self
You are destroying your Soul and your love of life

WAKE UP, WAKE UP AND LIVE AND LOVE
As you were intended to do.
Step out of the nightmare and the pain
Start up your heart and living again.

IT'S ALL GOOD!

-o-o-0-o-o-

Letter from my Angels

Our dearest one, you were brought to this
Earth to learn about Love and Acceptance.
Your whole life is about Loving and Accepting
Yourself as you are – a Human Being
With all the weaknesses of human life.

The only way you will be happy and
Joyful is to relate everything back
To these three words: -

LOVE AND ACCEPTANCE

Then you will be your True Self
In every respect
And able to get on with living authentically
As God intended you to live.

You are not and never have been selfish
You are not and never have been wrong
You are not and never have been living
Your life anything other than you intended
When you came to this Earth
You are not and never have been guilty
Of any sin
So put it right now by 'letting go'
Of this concept that you are wrong.

You will always be Right as far as
God is concerned.
Stop working and trying to get it
Right, for it is always right.
UNDERSTAND?
Your loving Presence
The God Within

MY ANGELS

They came to me in my time of need
When I felt alone and needed to be heard
They listened to my moaning and my cries of woe
They listened to my crying when I had nowhere else to go.

They loved me, caressed me and held me tight
They showed me the way through my Pain
They taught me to love and taught me to shine
They then told me to share it with you.

THE KEY

Ask them to listen, ask them to be there
Ask them to help you with <u>your</u> PAIN
But always remember if you really want to know
<u>You</u> have to <u>listen</u> to what they have to share.

They will share with you God's secrets and how to love Yourself
They will teach you how to be and not to do
They will teach you to be compassionate towards your Loving Self
And they will show you that you're important too.

They will teach you that God is Love
And loves you as you are
He doesn't want you to punish yourselves any more
Believing you are sinful and worthless in His Eyes
That is not what God's about, HE IS LOVE!

A loving parent wants the best and will give his children all he has
And that is what God offers us
Why cannot we receive
Think of the pleasure it gives <u>you</u> to give
But think also of the Pain you feel

When someone rejects what <u>you</u> give with Love
And that is what we are doing to God.

Acceptance is always the KEY.

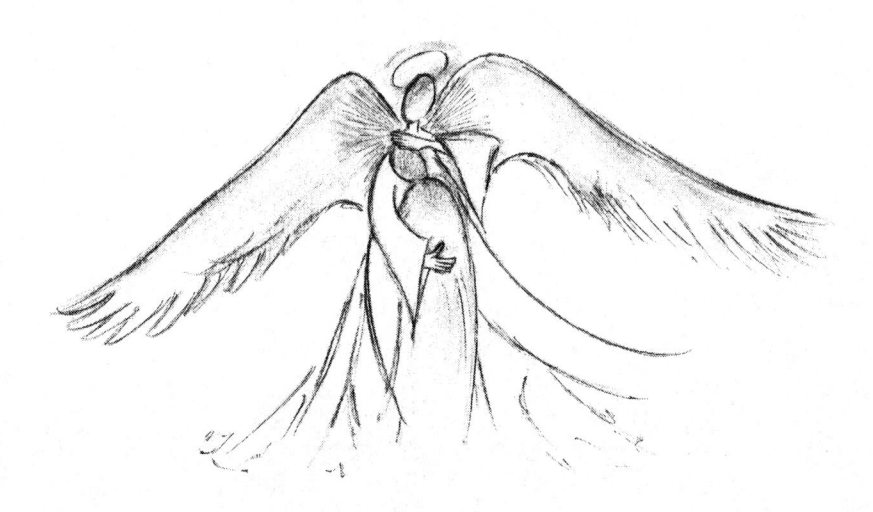

-o-o-0-o-o-

ALONENESS

This is the time when we connect with our PAIN
The Pain of the Soul as it tries to heal
And the feeling it seems we can never reveal
For it is something we Alone have to feel.

For those looking on and trying to help
You can only be There and be Strong
There is nothing to do and nothing can help
It's a journey we have to do ALONE.

It's a journey back to reveal our Truth
And see ourselves as we really are
And connect with God in a truthful way
Not pretending and hiding our darkness away.

The pain swallows us up and consumes us whole
It colours our life every day
Nothing ever goes right, or so it seems
So we have to stop and find another way.

There is only <u>one</u> way to heal this PAIN
And that is to go within
So just STOP and be QUIET and ask for help
In seeing your Truth and the lesson therein.

For those who are Humble and Open to Help
This process can be simplified
But most of us find it too hard to ask
What is it that Stops us, it's only our PRIDE!

Go out into Nature where all is well
Watch closely and you will see and hear
You are too busy my friend
You don't make the TIME

For yourself and for God who is your FRIEND.

You can keep the wound open
And keep picking away
'Til the hole gets bigger and bigger each day
and the Pain just gets deeper and harder to heal
for you never let go, and you never give in.

So my Friend just let go and let Love heal your Pain
Do not be afraid of the shadows you see
For hidden beneath all the darkness within
Are the seeds of new life just waiting to begin
Give your pain to God and be healed.

Underneath your greatest Fear is your greatest strength.

-o-o-0-o-o-

Excuses
(or reasons we give ourselves for not being Great)

Excuses. Excuses! I know them all
Not good enough
Not clever enough
Not tall enough
Not small enough
Not educated enough
Not good looking enough
Not articulate enough
Not artistic enough
Not brainy enough
Not worthy enough
Not acceptable enough
Not attractive enough
Not wise enough
Not intuitive enough
Not practical enough
Not clever enough
Not this, not that, the list is endless
Not a good enough background or upbringing
Boobs too big
Boobs too small
Belly too big
Bum too big

The excuses we use and the blame we dish out on the past, on the parents, on society as a whole
For who <u>we</u> are, for what we are, when the Truth is not ANY OF THIS. We're just plain SCARED OF OUR GREATNESS our 'Authentic Self', SCARED OF LIVING. Will I be accepted as 'I am'
Will I be Rejected again
And hurt as I once was before

So we stay with the Pain, but the PRICE IS TOO HIGH, it's your
Life you're not living for fear of getting it wrong
"Come on", "Wake up" says your Soul
What is there to lose?
Throw away your Fear and put on your Crown
Celebrate who you are for we all see you for real
So you cannot pretend any more
And pretending uses up all your Energy, your vitality too, and is not as attractive and magnetic as the Real Authentic You.
Being real is a magnetic quality which pulls success to you
So throw away your costumes and the roles you play
Say no excuses "today I will play ME"
As I was intended to be all along.
It's no effort, no big deal, we're all one and the same anyway.

-o-o-0-o-o-

LONELY

Yes, I do feel lonely sometimes when I'm sitting here on my own
And the world is busy around me
Families and couples seem everywhere,
But is only my Mind tricking me again.
For I am never really alone.
It is just that old feeling again.

So I listen to it, acknowledge its presence
Move into it deeper still
Accept that it's there and it loses its power
To spoil my day as before
For deep inside me I know I'm connected
With all people everywhere
Who are alone and share this feeling.

Also people within families or relationships
Or even in crowded places
Still feel lonely, so it comes from within
Where we share everything.

I sit with it for a few moments more
Then decide that the Love God gives
Me is ENOUGH to satisfy my every need
– I can proceed with my Day.

o-o-0-o-o-

Anger

Anger calls to us all the lesson to learn
The hurt passed down to us from the past
From generations of pain and sadness in the Soul
'Wake up' it says, 'do something about it'
Stop hiding it all in your FEAR
of not being accepted, and judged by it all.

Deal with the hurt and the pain that you feel
For it blocks the Love to your heart
And your family all suffers
So do it for them too

Heal your Soul and the Love will return
For Anger is necessary.
When its power is revealed
It stirs you to action within
Stand up for yourself and your own self-respect
And so let the Healing begin

-o-o-0-o-o-

ANGER (2)

Anger! This anger is all that I have
To provide me with answers to what lies ahead
It is wrong we are told to be feeling this way
When we ought to let go and ignore it today

But this anger will stay 'til I reach the end
Of my Role with my family and with my friends
This anger you see was a means to an end
And this end is now here, so let go and bend.

You will reap rich rewards in this world full of woe
If you listen to ME, don't hold on just LET GO
Your anger will serve you in only one way
And that is to punish you 'til your dying day.

-o-o-0-o-o-

PRIDE

This is the hardest one of all – where does it come from?

Pride goes before a fall they say,
but why is it there at all?
It is there to protect us from our sin,
but bend we must to be forgiven
If we let go and go within,
then all there is is truth and love
but pride keeps out unwanted guests
on our private side known only to us.
If we open it up this door that is shut
we can see just what is there
for only in loving and giving ourselves
do we get the chance to be healed.
What is it then this pride so strong!
It only serves to protect
To protect us from what? I ask myself
To protect us from the Truth
What is the Truth? I then ask myself
The truth is hard to bear
The truth is MY PAIN and FEELING ALONE
And it really is not fair …
that I have had no support in this life of mine
On this journey to love and light
Except from my Maker who is always there
In his arms he is holding me tight
And guiding me on with this great weight of mine
Right to the bitter end
But this journey my friend is the last
One I'll make for it really is the end – FOR ME.

-o-o-0-o-o-

BITTER FEELINGS

Bitter feelings are caused by our needs not being met
By those we expect to fulfil us
And by <u>giving too much</u> and not hearing ourselves
As we cry out in pain, "What about ME?"

But our cries go unheard as we turn a deaf ear
To our heart that is saying "let go
Of everyone else – just listen to <u>ME</u>"

"I need your Love and I need your care" – says your heart and your soul – "go within"
for until you feel fulfilled and happy within
how can you possibly help anyone else?

But the cry goes out "If I make them happy – I'll be ok" – but are you?
It's time for the TRUTH

No pretending, Be Real, what do you Really Feel
Are you really just Neglecting yourself
Come on, just be honest, no more denial my friend
For the Truth is there to be seen
In your reactions, your face, and your body
Tells all to those who have time to see

So acknowledge the truth "I am bitter"
Then you have the Power to Heal
And learn from this feeling for its showing you the way
Back to your Real self and the love and sweetness that you seek

Behind the bitterness lies the Sweetness
Seek and you will find the key.

-o-o-0-o-o-

BITTERNESS AND RESENTMENT

Bitterness and resentment all around me
There is nothing I have to do
But see it all and accept it all
And dissolve it all away.

This is the work of the Highest Power
This is what I came to do
To Heal my world and free it of pain
And all of its suffering too.

MESSAGE FROM GOD THROUGH MY HEART

I have given you the way
I have given you the Love
I have given you the Light and the Power

Now use it you must
No more doubt, no more fear
THIS IS WHAT YOU HAVE BEEN WAITING FOR.

-o-o-0-o-o-

WHEN WILL THE BITTERNESS END?
Between Men and Women

Bitter!! Not me my friend, there's no bitterness in me
I'm happy and so full of love
But the truth is all hidden in the sweetness and the pretence
That is not love, but denial my friend.

Not until you have faced your own darkness my friend
Will you come to the Love and the Light
For the Darkness is there, you have just turned away
For the Fear and the Dread that it brings

If only you knew that the Way to the Truth
Lies behind all the darkness inside
But we cannot accept it, we are Pure so it seems
But your thoughts say otherwise My Child.

Without Fear there's no Love, for it teaches us all
That the Power lies within not without
Without Darkness my Child your Seeds cannot grow
To blossom and reach for the Light

So face your Darkness and go within
What is worse than you already feel?
Your Demons and Dragons will all disappear
For they really are nothing, but Fear and Pretence
An illusion created to scare yourself more
By your subconscious mind
to make you move on
Out of FEAR INTO LOVE

FOR IN LOVE YOU CANNOT BE
IN FEAR ANY MORE.

-o-o-0-o-o-

Depletion

My battery is flat, I've given all that I can, emotionally, spiritually, physically, to ensure my family is happy. The rest is up to them, for I can give no more – there's nothing left for me. Time's running out and I have to keep within to Restore, Renew and Recharge, make a life for myself, no more sacrifice or pain – for I carry no anger, resentment, or bitter, jealous feelings in my heart, only love. I can't ease their pain, their grief, their life, this they must do for themselves as I have done – if not they too will carry the GUILT and the HURT of the past, passing it down to their children too – for the pain is passed on not by what is said or even acted out, but by the <u>unsaid thoughts and feelings</u> they carry in their <u>hearts</u> pretending all is well, yes I am, I'm just fine, they all say, but I know the Truth. I see the Truth. I feel what is held deep inside each and everyone's heart, for God has given me his Eyes to see that beyond this pain is the Beautiful Innocent True self if they could only let it Be free. When all the unsaid thoughts and feelings are brought to the Light of Day, they too will see what I can see, God in each one.
Love in each one.
Purity in each one.
And Life as it was meant to be Heaven on Earth
Paradise. Freedom for all.

-o-o-0-o-o-

REVENGE

Why do I feel the need for revenge?

YES, I do feel the need for Revenge sometimes
But I do not have the Power
To hit back at the ones who hurt me so
To attack them with my Hate

When I look at these people I can see
That I don't need to do this anyway
For if I look close into their eyes and their hearts
They already are feeling the pain within themselves
And attacking and hating and hurting within.

So why waste my time and my energy thus
Haven't I suffered enough?
For it's time to let go and get on with MY LIFE
And leave them to get on with theirs.

I refuse to carry the PAIN any more
And let <u>them</u> punish me this way.

Happiness is my Best Revenge
And I choose to say YES to LIFE

-o-o-0-o-o-

THE SPIDER'S WEB

I don't want to do this any more
This silly game they play
The game that causes family war
That sets us up against each other

The game that "<u>one</u>" controls to meet the needs they have!
Instead of being themselves, they spin a web to trap, deceive and slay
Their prey who, unsuspecting, crawls into their field of Power
Then snap into the jaws of hell
There's no escape this time

For you will pay me back in kind
For all I've done for you
This is the price you pay for my love
Pay up and win your prize!
The game's not over 'til you are all dead
And the one who's left gets it all

If you stay the course
If you do as you are told
The promise of that "love" will be yours
But if you fall from Grace then the Spider will pounce
And her venom eats away at your Soul.

-o-o-0-o-o-

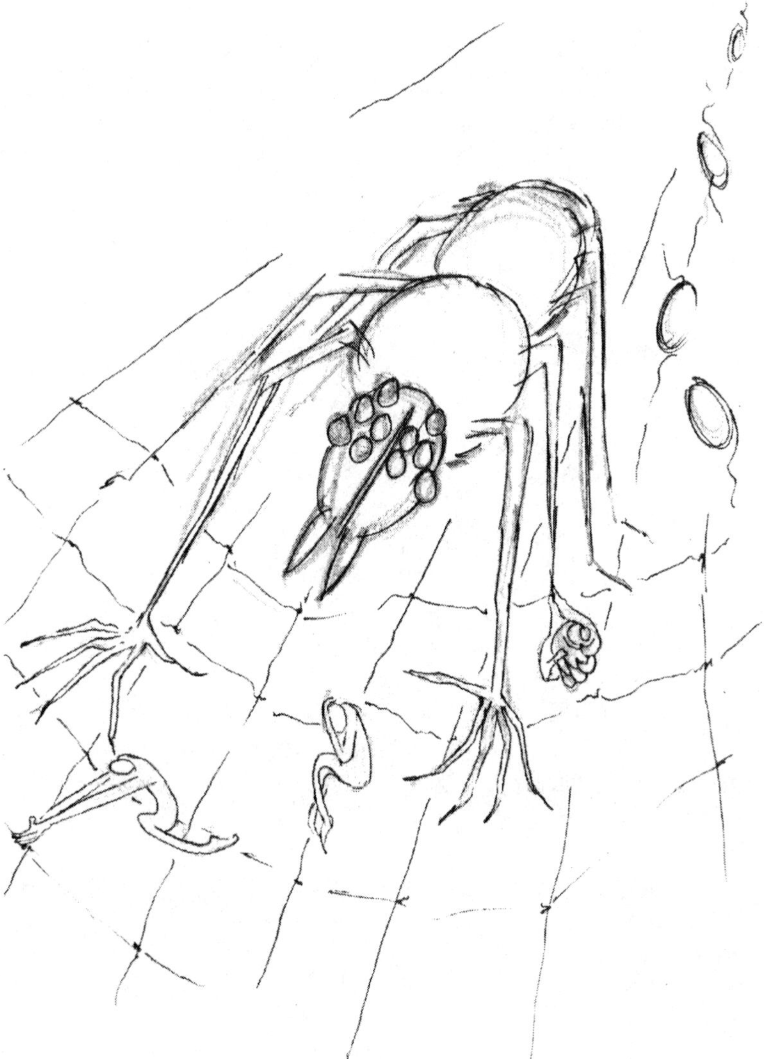

The Game's Over

It's time to begin again
To put down the past and the life I had
Let the Healing begin in a Powerful Way
Let the roses bloom and my garden flourish
With all I have planted and sown

For my Life has great meaning
And it's my life I know
To Live to the fullest I can
So I take up my role in the centre stage
Proud to be ME and let the world know!

That I'm back again, but the disguise has gone
And the Play is My Own and belongs to ME
No-one else can play this Part
So play on, let the music begin

The notes are sweet and as pure as can be
And the tune is authentic and comes only from me
For it's all I <u>know</u> to be happy and free
To encourage others as they struggle to be
The way we were intended by God
When He gave us this life on Earth.

-o-o-0-o-o-

I JUST WANT SOMEONE TO MAKE IT BETTER

I just want someone to make it better
I just want someone to take away the pain
I just want someone to take my hand again
So I don't feel so very much alone.

No-one to hold me tight
No-one to share my thoughts with
Sometimes this life of mine is so hard to bear
The tears flow so easily
My pen just keeps on going
But my heart knows I've had enough
And it's time to let go.

My family are all settled now
No-one needs me any more
Or so it seems, when I'm feeling low
I don't know where I belong any more.

Then God gives me another wake-up call
And tells me it's all as it should be
Then the darkness recedes once more
It's daylight again
And I go on   just BEING, but not DOING.

My DOING programme has gone
No more WORK as we know it on EARTH
For God makes it effortless and easy – just PLAY
BUT I HAVE TO GIVE IT UP FIRST.

Hand it over, let it go, stop thinking and working it out
Just do it, just live it, it's LOVE
That's what it's all about.

-o-o-0-o-o-

TIRED OF IT ALL

I'm tired and I've had enough of it all
What you may well ask?
Of Life? Of Living? Existing? Of Being?

NO! no! no! none of that, I love it all.

I'm tired and fed up with being told off
By the voice inside my head
That makes me wrong, that blames myself
For how I feel and how I act.

For being sick or feeling tired
Or just being wrong about it all
My heart screams out to me yet again
It's not your fault, you have done nothing wrong

You are here to learn what works and what doesn't
So the next generation can be set free
As you have freed yourself

FROM CONFORMING
FROM DOING
FROM GETTING IT RIGHT

SO YOU CAN SEE – IT'S ALL PERFECT – INCLUDING YOU
OPEN YOUR EYES TO GOD IN YOUR HEART.

Then your body will know what it's like once more
To feel comfortable and relaxed and have total peace
And the energy will be there for whatever you want
And whenever you want, as it flows once again
And your life is restored to how things were meant to be.

And the living is good

And you enjoy it all
No more struggle and pain
No more fighting to be free

Just surrender your control and let
God take over once again
And give you the life you deserve
Your balance restored and as it should be.
No more ups and downs just flowing with the flow
It's so easy when I just let go and be who I'm meant to be

MY SELF
MY DIVINE SELF

MY HOLY SELF
MY GODSELF

                    I AM

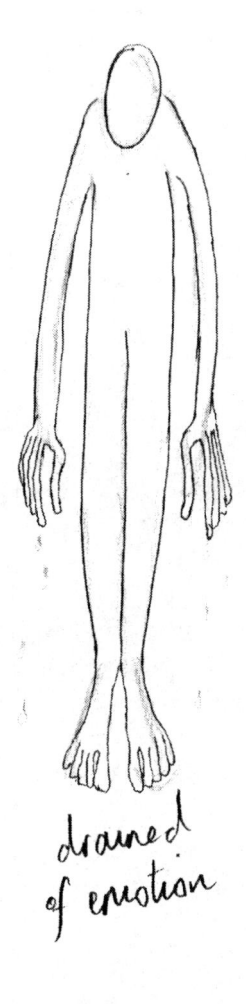

               -o-o-0-o-o-

drained of emotion

IT'S GETTING ON MY NERVES

It's getting on my nerves
These feelings in my body
The aching legs, the restless feelings
The stiff and aching muscles.

My body won't move how I want it to move
No energy, it's all gone – where? I don't know!
YES, I do know my body has had enough
Of the thoughts that do not serve me now
For it wants to be free once again as a child
To get up and go, be alive and be free
As we were all meant to be.

Not old and tired and feeling worn out
This is not how God intended it to be
This was our Control, we thought we knew best

But do we?

IS THIS LIFE
IS THIS LIVING
IS THIS WHAT WE WORK AND SAVE FOR
WHEN WE HAVE ALL OUR NEEDS MET AND THE MONEY TO SPEND ON OURSELVES

BUT WHAT'S THE USE OF IT ALL IF OUR HEALTH IS NO GOOD AND NO ENJOYMENT IS THERE – JUST WHAT IS THE POINT.

WAKE UP AND LOVE.

-o-o-0-o-o-

LIFELESS FEELINGS

Lifeless, this feeling persists
Although I know now it isn't true
My body is giving up, I cannot control it any more
Though my small thinking was that I could.
So I put it to God one more time and listened

Just BE HAPPY God says
And I'll do the rest
There is nothing more for you to do!
Your Life will just BE NOW
Your Burdens no more

FOR THE CONTROL IS NOW MINE NOT YOURS.

ENJOY IT ALL.

-o-o-0-o-o-

STOP THE BLAMING!

Stop the Blaming, stop it NOW

CUT IT OUT

IT'S YOU IT HURTS

IT'S YOUR SOUL IT DESTROYS

IT'S NOT YOUR FAULT

IT NEVER WAS

YOUR HEART BELONGS TO GOD

Take Responsibility only for Your Self. Don't interfere in other people's process. It just distracts you from dealing with your own.

-o-o-0-o-o-

It's not My Fault

It's not my fault
I am not to blame
For the life I have received
I have taken in
I have spat it out
I am sick and tired of it all.
We call it sin
And receive the blame
Dished out by those who have no soul
And the guilt goes on
And the game's played out
'til we walk away from it all
and leave them to their childish ways
– the childish games they play
and they call it "LOVE"
how dare they call it love.
How dare they say they care?
This is not care for they have no idea
what it means any more.
They just destroy themselves and others
in their fear and their manipulative ways of being.
And the world goes on
and the cries are not heard
– ignored by the noise of the game.
So all I can do is to stay with myself
my hopes, my dreams, my world
and hope one day they will wake up
to themselves
and their pain which is shared by all.

-o-o-0-o-o-

I REMEMBER

What do I remember? I remember it all
So very well now I am clear in my head
That I am here to have fun in the playground of Life
For that is where I am ME
No-one else, don't you see?

That is where we are free of the pressure to conform
And develop as we really should be
With each other, not those who are telling us how
"Be like this, just do that, listen to me" – "I am right"
But are they, these people who teach us
The ways of the world?
For when I see into their eyes
They are not happy and free,
They are sad and downtrodden
No Joy, no Peace, no Time, no Love

And these are the ones who tell us how to live
When they don't know how themselves
We the children of the world
Are not fools you know
We are not easily deceived by the adults around
We see their hearts and we try to help
With our simple childlike ways

But they won't listen,
They still shout and scream at each other!

-o-o-0-o-o-

THE FAMILY TREE

Our tree lies bare
With its branches hung low
Some rotting and dead to the core

No life at the top, or so it would appear
No leaves, just brown sticks all twisted and gnarled
And broken off in the storms of Life

But to see the '<u>Real Truth</u>' you have to see right inside
Deep down to the very core and its
Life and how it Began
To the Heart of all Life and the reason we're here

-o-o-0-o-o-

SOFTNESS
... for Myra

Softness is a cloud that touches our hearts
Like a gentle breeze on a summers day
It changes our outlook
And makes our world a gentler place to be

Like candy-floss and angels' wings
And butterflies and babies' skin
A feeling of wholeness and oneness with all
Descends like a second skin around the heart

And the heart unfolds its petals slowly
To receive the nourishment it so desperately needs
Let the sweetness begin as the bitterness dissolves
Without even a scar to show it was there

And a new beginning springs forth
From the well of desire
For Life to be Lived to the full once more
No more hardness, no more despair
Just Love from within created by Source
May Peace descend on all.

o-o-0-o-o-

CHOICE

It makes me sad to see the plight of some women today
Locked in their own little world afraid to speak up for themselves
Feeling they have NO CHOICE, but that is not true
For here am I to speak up for you!

You do have a CHOICE just listen and pray
And God will hear your call

It is time to stop sitting – it is time for Doing!
Let's have some action today!

It's EASY you see to be YOURSELF and let go of the image
behind the MASK.
YOU ARE SOMEONE SPECIAL!

-o-o-0-o-o-

which one is me?

COMPASSION

Compassion lifts the Soul to a higher plane
A much lighter and freer path
One that's guided by light not the darkness of fear
Based on Love and pure being
Not sadness and guilt

It comes only from God through the Light of the Soul
To enable us all to move on

Out of fear into Love
Out of darkness into Light
Out of desperation into TRUST

That we are all guided and cared for
By our Creator above all else
And we each do our part
Leave the rest to the Soul
Who knows what their journey's about

-o-o-0-o-o-

CONFUSION

Confusion reigns yet again in my head
And my heart is saying No just stop
Listen to me it says, listen well and just be
Then clarity will soon return again.

When my mind is busy and making me wrong
My body suffers in its wake
And my heart sings out from beyond MY SOUL
Hush it says, be still within, BE STILL.

For this is where my answers lie
Not "out there" in my striving and doing
My journey within and the magic it brings
Is the only way forward for me

I have it all in my grasp if I could just let go
Completely of any plan
And let God do it all and give me it all
Surrender again to my heart

But I'm letting them down my Fear taunts me still
In a very quiet but persistent voice
No you're not says my heart, no you're not, stop your thoughts!!
Just let them dissolve away
For you only know Love and the Truth is your way
THE ONLY ONE LET DOWN IS YOU.
DO YOU SEE?

-o-o-0-o-o-

COURAGE AND STRENGTH

It takes courage and strength to stand up for yourself
It takes courage and strength to stand alone
It takes Love and Truth to be Yourself
It takes Love and Truth to be with God

Stand up my Friend and do not Fear
Laugh at yourself and see who you are
For if you could see what I can see
You would <u>know</u> that you are a
Magnificent, Powerful Being of Light

-o-o-0-o-o-

A Direct line to God changes everything

TO BE OR NOT TO BE

This is the choice I am given by God
To live a life filled with peace and joy
Or one that is full of fear and woe
But the fight goes on with the voice in my head (Fear)
That is desperately struggling now to be heard

The volume you see has been turned down real low
So it's not being heard very often now
For my life is so peaceful and free of stress
Since I listened to God instead

This voice ruled my Life for most of my years
And only comes up now and then
To stop me moving on and being myself
In a world full of fear and despair

"Surrender" - God says – "just let go and let me
Take care of it all and set you free
To enjoy, to partake in the pleasure of it all
No more effort, no more struggle, only joy".

So again I release my so-called 'control'
And into the FLOW I go
Where to and how I do not know
But it's good to be back again

Back in the heart of God where
ALL IS GOOD AND RIGHT
WITH THE WORLD –
For, as God says, Nothing is IMPERFECT he's made

He wants only the Best, hear his Voice and just know
Peace on Earth will just FLOW, when we all believe this is True
So let go of your LIMITS and show your children the Way
To the Top of the Tree and the best of the fruit
No more fallens, or inferior stuff will do.

Expect it all and you will receive
All your needs and desires will be met
No more poverty in our hearts,
No more 'poor me' in our thoughts
No more sadness only joy will be yours
Trust my words, they are from God
And He will never let you down
For HE IS LOVE.

And Love is Richness and Abundance at its Best.

JUST BE YOU

-o-o-0-o-o-

THE WOW – the World of Wonder

Through the eyes of my child
I see the new ME unfolding petal by petal
Exposing My Self to the world of my new reality.
I see the Love and the Joy of who I really am
I see it flow out of me into all eternity
I watch it flow and it amazes me still.

I smile a quiet smile and take it all in
I see it all, I love it all, I revel in it all.
I AM THE SOURCE OF IT ALL
IT IS ALL ME.

My new journey is full of sweetness and bliss
No more struggle or pain
No more aching and longing to be free
For freedom is who I am
And Life is WHO I AM

My DOING flows from my BEINGNESS
WITH GRACE AND EASE
THIS IS THE ULTIMATE REALITY
THE LIFE I HAVE WAITED FOR
IT'S HERE NOW – I EMBRACE IT ALL.

-o-o-0-o-o-

CREATION

Creation as I see it is glorious and beautiful
The artwork of God as we all unfold
And show ourselves Truly, Exposed to the world
As we really are
Forgetting the judgments and heartaches of old
Forgetting the hurt and the pain
As we remember once more how loved and special we all are
How unique, how different, how resourceful we all are
In meeting our needs in a human way
'til we remember <u>we</u> don't have to meet our needs
they are already met from within
and our lives are planned out and the story unfolds
showing more of the picture and more of the Truth

Who am I? I remember, I know who I am
I remember it all and the Great Big Plan
And the vision we hold and the <u>Lie</u> that was told
Of the sin and the falling from grace.

IT'S NOT TRUE. WE ARE LOVE

We are Whole and Complete as we are.

-o-o-0-o-o-

CREATING AND CREATION
COMMITMENT TO SELF

You create your world by your thoughts
You think, by your beliefs and by your
Choices you make

If you do not like your world then
Change it by changing your thoughts
Beliefs and choices it is as SIMPLE AS THAT

What gets in your WAY IS JUST FEAR
And all FEAR IS, is Imagination of
What might happen, based on past experiences

What you expect you will often get, so start
Expecting what <u>you</u> really want to happen

If you don't go Within yourself you
Will <u>never</u> get what you want from your outside world.

If you are <u>not going within</u> you <u>are going without</u> – it's up to you
No-one else can change your world
<u>Not</u> your partner, your family,
Your friends or anyone else BUT YOU.

If you are not investing in Yourself
Then you will receive nothing – you
Will receive back only what <u>you</u> invest!

Financially, Health wise, Love, Peace, Joy, BEAUTY.

If you are not investing and committing to you
Then you have <u>not</u> a self to share

You <u>cannot give</u> what you do not already have or own yourself – you have given it away and the emptiness has to be filled by you.

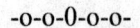

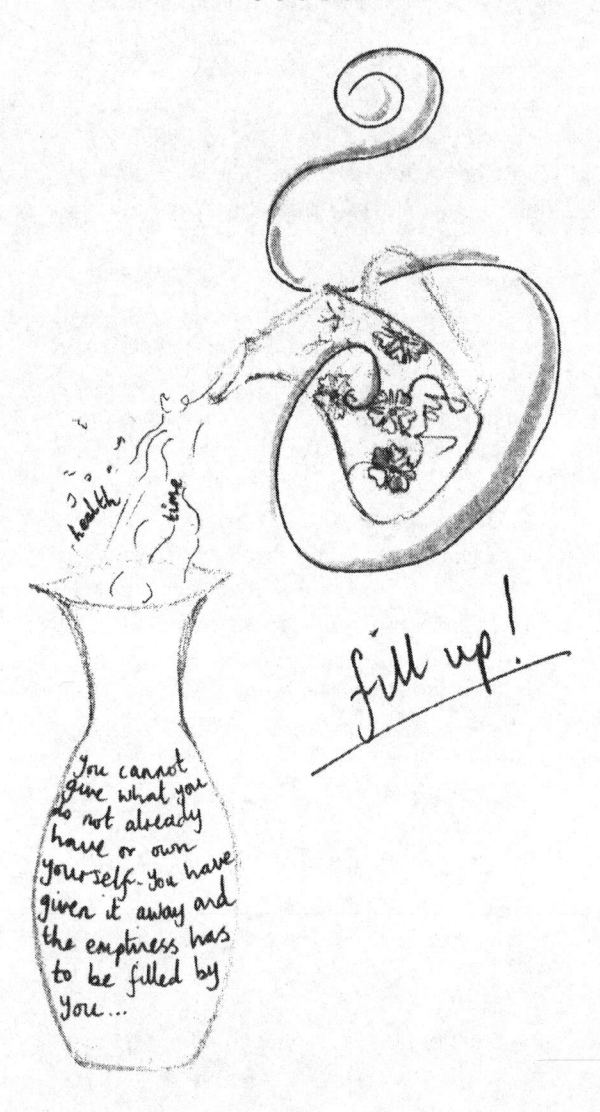

-o-o-0-o-o-

DENIAL…

… is not listening to your True self
It is listening to the World of Fear.

When you make yourself wrong for who and what
You are (you are making God wrong too)
You are denying the Truth

And the Truth, my Child, is always there
But you cannot see it and feel it
When your eyes and your heart are closed

And you are switched off to the Light and the Love
That God is giving you
"I am Right" is all I hear you say
but you are <u>wrong</u> in the eyes of God.

For your Right is not the same as God's
Your right is only your pride
You cannot see that the Dark is there
And that is where <u>you</u> hide!

"What is the dark?" I hear you ask
The dark is only your fear
But you will not listen to me my Child
When I call you to the Light

For you are answerable to God
Not just by your words and deeds
But by your <u>Thoughts</u> as well
And what are those thoughts you so deny?

Your Anger, your bitterness, your hate, your lust,
your control for Power and Money,
Success and Greed

And lack of Trust that God provides
When you are humble, meek and mild.

So come to God in <u>all</u> your Truth
In all your nakedness not your disguise
Then God will hear your cries my friend
And will lift you up and heal your pain.

-o-o-0-o-o-

Process (1)

My process was hard and I had to commit
To my "Self" again and again
In order to Learn all the shortcuts to God
So that others may gain from my Life and my Living
And my pain.

I feel so blessed and am privileged to serve
In the only way that I know how
And that is by Loving and giving My Self
Now I know I have a full self to give

And what is the "Self" you may well ask
And I will tell you this
It is what is left when you have stripped away
All the pretence, all the games we play
When your heart is healed and you no longer have pain
And this process takes some time
The "I AM" is all that is left
And All there is and ever was
And you feel completely whole again.

-o-o-0-o-o-

DEPRESSION

Depression's a way of hiding myself and
Meeting my needs from within
I'm hurting, I'm angry, I'm fearful again
So escape is the only way.

When I'm in it, it feels as if everything's wrong
With my world and with what I am doing
But I'm clever you see for my Soul knows the way
To wholeness and acceptance again.

I wallow and pity "<u>poor me</u>" once again
Why doesn't everyone see
How hurt I am
How insecure I am
Wake up my Soul says and really see
<u>The belief</u> that creates your Reality.

I believe I'm not good enough
Not worthy of it all
I've told myself so many times I now
Believe it to be True.
Not so, says My Soul
Wake up and really see You are the
Creator of it all. You choose to
Experience it all so you can grow
Look back and see how you've grown
And moved on
You're not so small any more
Accept your Power, your Magnificent
Self and show it to the World.

The darkness is just a place in your mind
You create when things are too much
But your mind is your own, no-one fills it but you

Download says your Soul, put the past in the Bin
Delete, get rid, end it all
Put in what you want now, re-focus it all
It's not then, it's NOW and the
Power is yours to change your mind
To change your view
To change your world
Put in a new Program

I believe in Me
I trust in Me
I love and Accept Me as I am Now, all of me
For I am worthy to have a Life I love,
Just because I am HERE ON EARTH.
It's my Right.
Without the dark you don't see the Light.

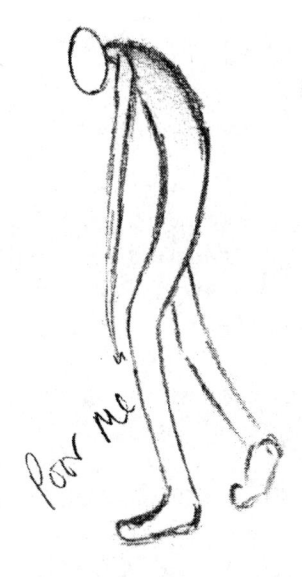

-o-o-0-o-o-

IT'S NEVER ENOUGH – Dissatisfied

I look around me and such beauty I see
I have all the freedom in the world for me
I have enough money, enough food, enough time
But there's something missing from this life of mine

I can't work it out – it's so deeply ingrained
In our consciousness from times gone by
There's so much to do and so much to be
I don't recognise 'my self' any more.

So many changes have taken place
So many beliefs and thoughts I've let go
There's no-one to be and there's nowhere to go
So what is the purpose of it all?

So I put it to God as I always do
And ask for the answer to be given to me
In the simplest terms and the easiest way
For simplicity is God's way "they" say.

What is out there and who are they?
My inquisitive mind wants to know
Are they real are they thoughts going round in my head?
I need to know, God, now, please tell me all.

So I asked God to write me a letter to say
The Truth of it all in clear words
And this is what he dictated and I wrote down
For this explains it all .....

Letter to me from God Within:

Dear Heart,
You are all there is and more
You are all that ever will be
You are everything that was and is
You are what you are because
You are ME
You Live your Life untouched by the world
You live your Life in Love with all you see
You live your Life by the Truth of it all
And the Truth of it all is all you see.

ME

I am only Responsible for Me.

-o-o-o-o-

My heart in God's heart, and God's heart in Mine.
Oneness with MY GOD.

Me: So I'm more than enough and I'm all there is?

God: Does it make sense? Am I coming through?
Are <u>you</u> receiving it all? For I'm giving it all
The rest is up to you

To Receive all I give
To Let go and just be
A channel of Love, Peace and Joy
To show up in this Life, let me do the rest
And the Flow will be restored to all

-o-o-0-o-o-

<u>GUILT</u>

Guilt is a nightmare that keeps me awake
My body can't rest and my mind won't be still
"It's my fault" – it says, as I try to relax
it must be, whose else can it possibly be?
if something's not right, then I've done something wrong
or so it would seem to me.

The quiet voice in my head says: "Relax, think of love
Let go of <u>your need</u> to be right
Your Light is so bright and the world needs your LOVE
Why hold back, think of me and LET GO".

Your soul is so hungry for Love, don't you know
And your heart will be full once more
If you let in the Love and the Light that God brings
Hear him knocking and open the Door

Your star is awaiting for you to alight
And carry you off on your tour of the Night
And you will remember your purpose in life
And the Gifts you came to bring.

Be at Peace My Friend.

-o-o-0-o-o-

TENDERNESS – To My Friend

Today I feel scorned by myself, no-one else
My eyes feel heavy and full of tears
For the hardness I've shown over the years
Not to anyone else, but to myself
I deserve a little Tenderness.

The hardness, it seems, goes on and on
And there is no release for this heart of mine
My Pain is still there, well hidden below
For the stuff of Life has covered it well.

But heal I must this Heart of mine
For my family tree needs to grow and grow
In Love not Fear, by Living and Being
So this Time I give the Love to Myself
And my inner child who bore the pain,
Now deserves the best I can give
And she will be re-born again
To move into the Light and Love of God
Out of the Fear and the Strife of the
Earth Bound Plane

So this is the message I give to Myself,
BE GENTLE, BE LOVING, BE KIND,
BE TENDER, BE TRUE,
BE ALL TO YOURSELF …
and the Love of God will come through
with Grace and the Miracle
he has promised you,
but first you must obey and
Love yourself with all your heart.

Then the pain will go away
and you will be
HEALED.

Together we have shared our pain and together we will heal!

-o-o-0-o-o-

*"Be gentle, Be loving, Be kind,
Be Tender, Be True,
Be all to yourself"*

"but heal I must this heart of mine"

I AM FREE!

The secret of happiness is to let go of all my thoughts and <u>I am HAPPY</u>

I feel light and free in my heart
Free to be who I want to be
No strings attached to me
I can go where I want
Be who I want to be
Say what I want

I accept myself as I am
I celebrate who I am
What I am and why I am here

I know my True Purpose in Life
And that is to be Happy, to be ME and let go of everything.

I hand the controls over to my God self and set myself free
This is a truly wonderful feeling

NOTHING and NO-ONE has any Power or CONTROL over ME.

-o-o-0-o-o-

GRACE

Grace comes to us from God, when we are ready and willing
To see with our hearts, not our eyes
What Living's about, no more doubting or fear
Just Heaven on Earth for us all.

Let go of old ways and patterns of being
Just be yourself, as you are
No more pain, no more Fear
No more struggle, no more past
Just let Go – God sees to the rest.

-o-o-0-o-o-

Let go and Let God

THANK YOU GOD

Thank you for my Power and my Strength
Thank you for all my help
Thank you for all I have and all I see
Thank you for the Beauty all around and within me
Thank you for the love I receive and the love within
Thank you for the VOICE I have
Thank you for finding ME.

For the ME I now see is Really ME
The one I have hidden for so long
And this ME is now totally free
To fly with the birds and soar with the clouds

Thank you for colours in my life
Thank you for the Light and the Dark
Thank you for the Fears and the Doubts I have felt
Thank you for the Sadness and Anger too
For without all these I would not have learned
The lesson I came here to learn
And that is to love with all my heart
MYSELF AND THE WORLD
And this LOVE is the POWER I now wish to use
To heal those who need my help
For this Power's so great and is Magical you see
Thank you for my size, so much have I grown
Not just in my body but my MIND
Can this person I see really be ME
Am I really that BIG and LARGE AS LIFE
YES I am, I just haven't wanted to see it,
I have hidden myself behind my shell, YET AGAIN!

-o-o-0-o-o-

HUMILITY

Humility is a gift from God when we have healed our inner child and can connect again with Him on a new level of understanding.

Being humble isn't easy, we feel, because it makes us wrong, and we don't know how to deal with that for our lives don't make sense if we cannot be right on what we know and do at different times in the process we call healing.

The layers do have to go and each one brings new insights and newer levels of where we are.

But the process demands us to see ahead to the good and better times for, if we didn't, we couldn't go on to discover who we are.

So if I've been right too many times, it is because <u>I know</u> that deep inside me I can be healed and now I know this is so.

How do I know, you may well ask, when I have <u>known</u> before. I know because God has promised me and He never lets me down. I know because inside of me is a heart connected with Him and that heart is now strong and whole again and I have atoned for my sin.

I have forgiven my inner child for blaming herself so much.

-o-o-0-o-o-

RESISTANCE

What is it I'm resisting
No get up and go, no moving on
It seems my life is standing still
No energy at all.

My body feels lifeless deep inside
My soul calls out to be still, do not move.
Stay with the feeling, do <u>not</u> Resist
And all will be revealed.

But I have so many days like this – my mind calls out
I want to move on, I want to <u>DO</u>, I cannot be still
The world is calling, I know not WHY
But obey, I must, my Soul insists and
So another day goes by and I sit here my body lifeless
And the Meaning becomes clear

This is MY CREATIVE SPACE, where I create my world in a different way
So surrender I must and let go of doing
And acting upon the stage
My <u>role</u> is <u>different</u> now.

I AM THE PRODUCER, THE CREATOR, THE CONDUCTOR
of this play we call life
So let go and have some fun
What do I want my world to be
My heart ticks on and whispers to me

Only the Best is yet to come, accept nothing less
For why would I want anything less
This time is so important now I see
This is the space I have created for me
To be quiet and go within

Let the work begin, let God's pen flow
Where do I begin – with MY WORLD!

Let's go back to the beginning when time began
And God's plan was a thought, an idea
'Make a World' was the Plan where life could be lived

through you, not by you, as you once thought
was the way it had to be
for I am the Source of the good and the bad
and it's how I intended it to be

for you to learn the lessons of life
and to be restored to the Whole
for you thought you were separate and all alone
when in fact you are not <u>you are ME</u>.

This applies to you all each and every one
You are all an aspect of me
A spark of Light and of Love in the fullness of time
And part of my Divinity

If you only knew how I loved you all
And would give you all I have
You would experience life as it was meant to be
Pure joy, pure bliss, pure being – ME

So put down your cares and be 'carefree' my child
For you now know it all – there's nothing to be
There is nothing to do and nowhere to go
You just are what you are and the answer Is <u>you</u>
There's no more mystery to unfold
No more clues, no more seeking
No more searching for Love
For you are the Source of it all.
GOD.

A LIFE LIVED IN Love not in Fear
So the world was created and Awesome it was
The Master design was so good, almost perfect it seemed
Everyone working together and being as one
'til man got too clever and tried to be GOD
take control of his own life and said he knew best
changed the blueprint for good and the disasters began

in came greed and then the pain as the HURTING BEGAN.

-o-o-0-o-o-

...changed the blueprint for good and the disasters began in came greed and then the pain as the HURTING BEGAN.

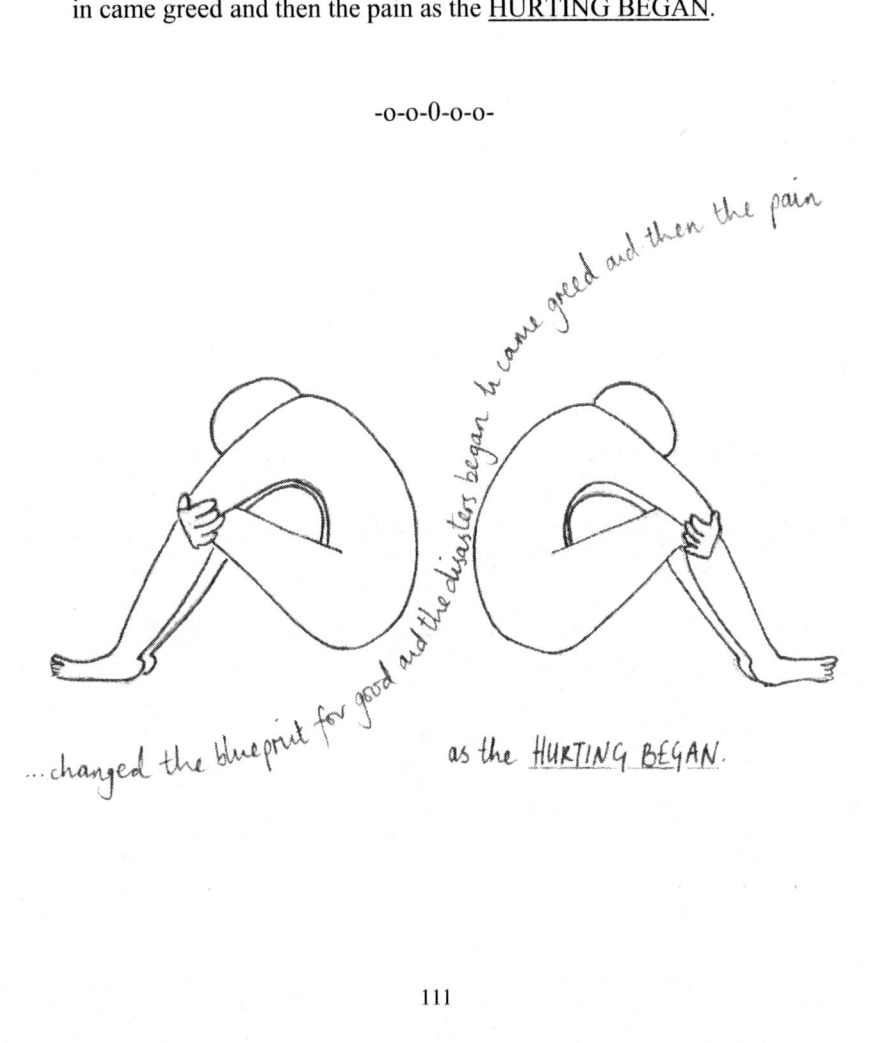

IRRITATIONS (Divine Interruptions) to listen

Children are "Divine Interruptions"

These come along when I cannot let go
And just trust in the presence of life
It's God saying to me STOP, listen and go within
You're in too much of a hurry my child

What I've planned for you is <u>so much more</u>
Than you could ever foresee
So let go of your doubts and your fears once again
Hold my hand. Walk with me and your life will be
So wondrous and beautiful and true
As I intended it to be.

For Creation is yours, a gift I bestow
On the rich and abundant in love
Your rewards will be great, far beyond your belief
For I have promised that this is so.

And my Promise will hold good for as long as it takes
For you all to come home to me
For it's where you belong and it's where you are headed
The rest is all up to me.
Just walk the journey
Just turn up, say your piece
Then move on and let Me do the work

No more effort and strain
No more struggle and pain
Just pure joy in the nectar of life
This is how it will be for the ones now on Earth
If they will only listen to me

Put down your tools and take up your heart

Go within and listen to my Voice
For I love you so and want only the best
For my children who carry the light
To the ones in the darkness who've forgotten how to shine
And have lost their way to the JOY
And the Peace within – hold their hand
Give them love and a blessing from me
Then creation will be yours again.

Heaven on earth will take place as I promised you all
A life so good – a dream come true
When you work together for the good of all
The battle of Love will then be <u>WON.</u>

-o-o-0-o-o-

LETTING GO INTO JOY

Letting go of everything when it has happened
Is a wonderful thing
Letting go, moving on, clear your mind and stay free
That is all we have to do to live in Peace
What is "IS" – it won't change, just
Let go and say "what next?"
Is the way to find joy in your life
Letting go, putting down, don't hold on, move along
You cannot carry the weight any more
For your shoulders are tired and your body feels worn out
Just let go, just let go, put it down

No more pressure I'm told
No more carrying the load

It's God's job not mine any more

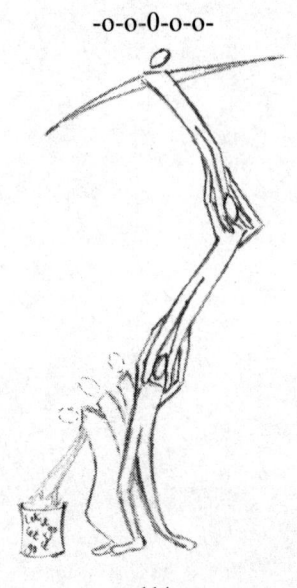

-o-o-0-o-o-

LIMBO

'Betwixt and between', they used to say
For this feeling we cannot describe
Confused, bewildered and unfocused with it all
This is the time for surrender

Put it all down and let it all go
Give it all up to God
For this is the time when we've done all we can
And the rest we can leave to Him

The Big Picture unfolds of what it's about
When we give up control and let go
But the feeling it brings is out of control
And we don't like that feeling at all.

And the Fear pulls us in as our heart says <u>NO</u>
Just wait and let life BE what it is
And I struggle against it, but fight it I can't
"Let it go", says my heart, "let it go".

Just accept where you are and the feelings you have
Be yourself, love it all and you'll see
The outcome you desire from your heart will come true
And all will be well again for you.

-o-o-0-o-o-

What a Relief

Oh what a relief it is to feel
As I was meant to feel
To be myself and to just let go
The waiting is all over
My Soul restored to its rightful place
My energy all comes back
My heart sings out in joy at last
I'm free, I'm free, I'm ME.
And the sweetness pours in
What a Blessed release
What a marvellous joy is Life
Not stifled and smothered by others' grief
Just alive at last, no more deadness within
No more grief passed down from the souls of the past
No more jealousy and fear or bitterness
Only love fills my heart and I can sing once more
No more Pain, no more struggle
Let the Healing just cease
As I respond to my heart and the Love of My God
And my Trust in Myself is now fully restored
So Live Your Life, Live it as God intended,
Be Yourself,
No-one else
JUST BE YOU

-o-o-0-o-o-

The Old Ways Hang On – BUT THE RIVER MUST FLOW

The old ways hang on, but no longer serve
It is time to grow and move on
They were right at the time, we <u>accepted</u> it all
But the world moves on and the River has to Flow.

If we don't we stagnate in the mud of the past
And the river insists it is time to let go
We can do as we wish now, not as we are told
But the freedom scares us so!

With a heart full of love
And a voice that's sincere
We can share with the world what we've learned
But it's up to them all to find their own way,
And the Path for themselves.

With a heart full of Love
We <u>can show</u> them our Way
But not lead them on lest they fall
And we fall down too, what good are we then
To the rest who are following too?

After struggling and stumbling like someone who was blind
I now know there's a better way
Just listen my Friend within, not without,
For that is where <u>your</u> answers lie

In the dark of the Soul where the secrets are hidden
You will find your own path full of light
And never look back to the times full of sorrow
For you <u>know</u> when you have got it right FOR YOU!

-o-o-0-o-o-

Let Down

If only you knew what it means to us all
When <u>you</u> don't take care of yourself
The sadness and pain and the hurt left behind
Is a hole in the heart of the world

If only you saw the damage you've done
Before it's too late to be healed
Just wake up and remember the reason you're here
And the gift you were meant to give
To those chosen by you and the ones you hold dear
Time ticks on and the wound needs to heal

Look around you and see what your life is about
The Truth's there and it's plain to see
Wipe the dust from your eyes
Heal the pain in your heart
And move on with your life as it was meant to be.

Step out of conformity and the need to please
Don't you see, that's not what it's about
Listen carefully, to your heart and the still small voice
That says STOP what you are doing
To yourself and the world that loves you so
For your heart is hardened and you've lost the plot

This is not how it was meant to be
Just remember, just listen to the loving and the wise
Find the key to your heart and your life once again
Restoration is all that you need
Peace and stillness will help but you have to commit
To your life and the ones that you love
Put love before pride and remember your dream
And your vision of how it should be

It's not love if it hurts
It's not love if there's pain
It's pure neediness, and the child within
Needs your love and acceptance of its innocence
Your spirit is Pure and you don't have the right
To make yourself guilty as hell

Stop, listen to God who speaks to you through
Those all around you and telling you the Truth
Stop being right, just let go and BE YOU AS YOU ARE
For that is all you have to do
Nothing else, no more SHOULDS –
We love you so.

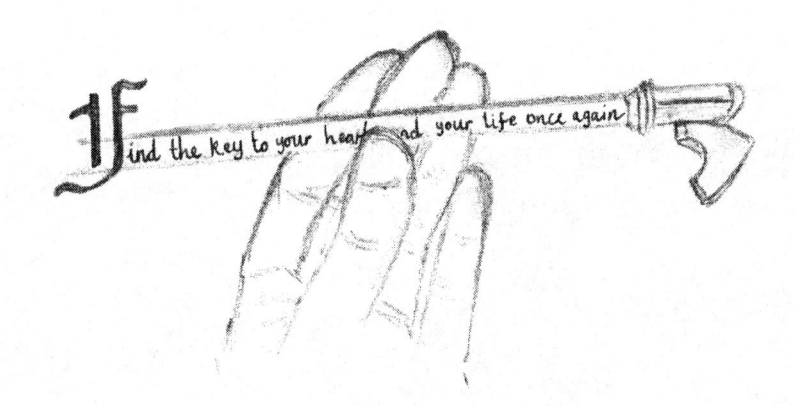

-o-o-0-o-o-

Find the key to your heart and your life once again

FREEDOM?

I feel like a bird that's been let out of its cage
Wanting to fly, but held back!
It's as bad as being trapped in that cage and I know I
Need to flap my wings and go, but what then?
What will <u>they</u> think, will <u>they</u> be hurt, will <u>they</u> be sad, will <u>they</u> be alone?

But <u>they</u> are already alone in their own sadness and grief,
Their pain and suffering, so why worry?
My flying will not change them or their feelings,
Will not add to their sorrow, their pain.
Their pain is their own not mine!

What stops me from flying, I do not know,
But I know I have to go,
To flee this nest where I have been <u>safe</u> for so long.

<u>SAFE</u> – but what is safe, is it happiness?
NO it is restriction, limitation, restraint and my Soul longs to be free
I long to be ME
So I can sing and shout in Joy
Encouraging others on their Path to Freedom.

What is <u>FREEDOM</u>?
It is <u>love</u>, it is <u>light</u>, – it's soaring with the birds
It is being Me to the full
Let me fly, let me fly, let me go
Let me soar to the Heights
I WILL … I WILL

<u>They</u> are not holding me back – it's me, it <u>is</u> me!!
Why? Of what am I afraid?

What is this <u>FEAR</u> that still limits me so?

Being wrong in the sight of <u>others</u>
Letting <u>them</u> down

But what about me? Am I letting me down?
YES! YES! YES!

And if <u>I'm</u> feeling let down, then I <u>will</u> let others down, this I know to be TRUE

So I release this FEAR with love to set me free
FREE IS WHAT I AIM TO BE

Free to love and be loved, for in the end that's all there is –

LOVE
LOVE
LOVE

free to be who I want to be — o-o-o-o-o- attached
No strings to me

YOU ARE ENOUGH

'You are enough as you are' God has drilled into my heart
'In just being yourself as you are'
And it's tired, I am now of arguing and being right
For God's love is the Ultimate Force in my life
That drives my heart and my body as one

I let go of the wheel and just relax
The journey of Life carries me on
And the Slow Lane is fun
And the scenery's good

No more crashing and thrashing around
For God sees more clearly than I ever could do
"Move over" – he says – "let me drive"

I am totally free, in my heart and my soul
And the Beauty I see inspires me so
I can lift other's spirits and help them
Hear the call of their own Soul
If they are willing and asking for help

For it's not what I do that counts
But who I am and why I'm here
So this RULE MUST APPLY TO US ALL.

God Bless

-o-o-0-o-o-

Let's Begin Again

If I had my time over what would I do?
Would I do it all over again?
Are there things I would change?
Are there things I'd let go?
What is it I have gained
From this Time here on Earth?

Many things have I learned
On my journey this time
And the main one I think is 'LET GO'
Of the plan in my mind and the need to conform
And also the Need to grow
For what I have realised, it's taken some time
Is that God does it all, grows me, grows you
With no effort involved, no energy spent
All I have to do is BE and ENJOY
What is given to me

                                          {BY LIFE
These are one and the same   {BY LOVE
                                          {BY GOD

-o-o-0-o-o-

SLEEPLESSNESS

3 a.m. The Lesson to <u>Trust</u>

I'm here again with my pen in my hand, unable to sleep for what is happening in my body. I don't really know why, but the feeling is strong and the longing and aching for myself to come home and be at Peace. "Let go", God says, "let go and rest". But the turmoil goes on deep in my chest, to find some answer to this body of mine that feels alien to me and uncomfortable most of the time.

I cannot rest easily, I know not why, for it's my unconscious mind at work again.

Let go, let go, let go and <u>TRUST</u>.

-o-o-0-o-o-

THE OPPOSITE OF TRUST –ANXIETY AND WORRY

The opposite of Trust is worry and anxiety (in other words FEAR AND FEELING ALONE).
Worrying is not Trusting your Self to cope with life situations.
Not trusting others to cope without you.
And not trusting in Life (God) to take care of you on your life journey.
Worrying over others can make them feel more insecure and inadequate to cope without you, particularly if they are feeling low. It does not teach them to meet their own needs and to trust in themselves when you are not around.

ALL IN ALL IT WEAKENS EVERYONE

The REAL TRUTH is we are part of a High Intelligence System and are extremely Powerful with the ability to change our world for the good of all.

THE TRUTH SETS YOU FREE!

It is our True Nature to Trust.

-o-o-0-o-o-

DRIFTING AIMLESSLY – I FEEL LIKE A ROBOT WITH THE WORKINGS REMOVED

I find myself just drifting alone
No path, no programme, no life
Alone, weary and aimless, all pleasure denied
An empty vessel with no purpose
Or so it seems.

My plan's washed away
Nowhere to go, no-one to be
Lost in the crowd of this place we call Earth
My spirit just longs to be free.

Free of the suffering, free of the pain
There's no pleasure any more in the material world
Is this what DEATH feels like
No life any more
No more wanting, no more expecting
No more anything.

I've deprogrammed myself
From all I've been taught
So what's left in this shell of a mind
My feelings are numb
I can't taste, I can't smell
I can't connect with the world any more

So I hide myself away
And just watch from inside
Life is passing me by
I don't know any more
I can't think any more
I just want to know WHY?

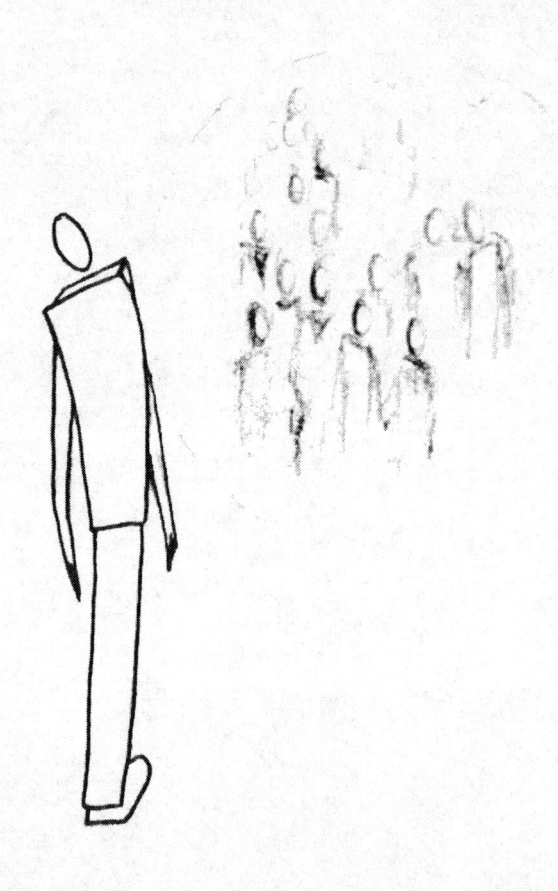

-o-o-0-o-o-

Letting Go

The Blueprint is There

Letting go and surrendering all your cares and concerns
To your God within
Will bring you Peace of Mind and Joy once more
Give them all away your Family, your Friends
Let go of healing them all
Let go of fixing everyone else
This is your final call

Wake up and remember Who You Are
Wake up and remember why You Are Here
You are here to Create a life of your own
And to find all the bits of yourself you have given away
All the bits that create your whole
For until you find your whole self again
You don't get to play THE PART
God has designed you for

And what is that part you ask My Friend I will tell you all
The part is yourself as you truly are
And not the role you have chosen through your fear
Your Ego (fear) has played its part
For it has shown you **HOW NOT TO BE**!
Let go of the Fear
Let go of the Goals
For it hasn't worked out so far
It is keeping you stuck
With the "stuff" of the past and the child you once were
But the "stuff" stays inside until you let go
And let your God decide
What is Right for you
What is best in your Life
What you have been designed specifically for

Only you will know that when you ask My Friend
And ask you must for your Life will depend
On the answers therein, not in the world out there
Where all is Fear and total despair

So go inside where it's quiet and still
And Ask and Listen and Wait and Let Go
Then the answers will come Believe me they will
And your Life will work out as it's meant to do
The Plan is there, the blueprint's inside
And you can search and search 'til the end of your days
In the outside world, but it isn't there

You can work and struggle and strut your stuff
And say to the world look at me
But the world doesn't care about you and your stuff and your pain
For it has enough of its own to bear

And the nightmare goes on and on in the dark
In the corners of your darkest mind
So Wake Up, this is your call, put on the Light
Stand up and walk tall on the path
Shake off the mud and the dirt of the past
And walk on the higher ground
Encouraging others to do the same
Do not get stuck in the 'Game of Blame'
For blaming others and everything out there
For what <u>you</u> are creating is Yours
Based on your Beliefs, no-one else's My Friend

Change your Mind	-	IT'S YOUR MIND
Change your world	-	IT'S YOUR FUTURE
Change your Life	-	IT'S YOUR LIFE

Into one that is Special, Unique and Your own
Take up the Responsibility for your life
See the gift that you've been given

The Beauty
The Love
The Nature of it all is there for you to enjoy
Open your Eyes, stop dreaming, the nightmare is over

You are and always have been Fully Equipped to handle
everything in your Life. You have just forgotten this is so!
(RESPONSIBILITY means the Ability to Respond, not as we
often interpret it to be <u>Feeling</u> responsible for)

For it is not out there, it is all within you
And you hold the key to your life, not me, says God

I give you a Life
I breathe into you your first breath
What you do from then is up to you
You can choose the way of Fear and playing your games
Or you can choose to be you and join
In with the fun of Life in a childlike way

-o-o-0-o-o-

REJECTION

Rejected, not loved by the one from whom you expect the most
Rejected, not seen or heard or respected too
My heart pours out to the one I have loved most
To the one who gave me my life
But my love is pushed back and rammed down my throat
Not acceptable, not good enough, I feel
Sometimes God I feel if I acknowledge the Truth
I will be left standing bare to my very soul
And my life it seems has been all wrong
But the mystery has to be solved

The mystery you see is it's all within me
And it's ME whose rejection I feel
Just leave ME alone, let me be by myself
No-one cares, is that how I feel.

Just because of one woman, whose job is well done
If only she had eyes to see
That her purpose in life was just to give birth
And provide me with lessons to learn

But my heart cries out loud
I want more, it isn't enough
To be dumped on this earth and let go
What is wrong with me, what have I done
This is not how it is meant to be

There must be more to my life
My heart cries in its pain
There must be more than this sadness and loss
No more she says, I have none to give
But the truth will always remain

She has it to give but just will not

Let go and give what she has come to give
Her gift to the world and her heart and her love
So she childishly stamps her feet and refuses to give
Because no-one has given to her
And so it goes on down the family tree
Refusing and feeling so sad
At her own loss and her pain which
She cannot reveal.

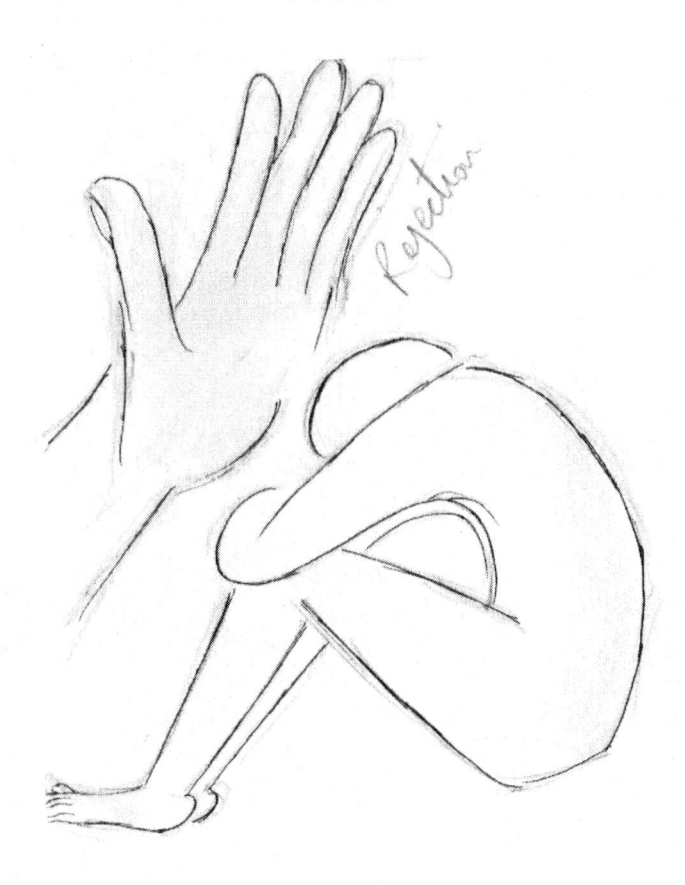

-o-o-0-o-o-

LETTING GO

Letting go of the things we love most and the People we love is a difficult process but, if we do not, we can never be our True Selves and experience love as it should be.

This doesn't mean not caring or loving people (as we Fear). It means just taking good care of ourselves and being totally Responsible <u>only</u> for us in order to Feel Unconditional Love in its purest form.

Maybe love would be easier if society had not taught us to put everyone else's needs before our own.

Maybe then we would not be so Resentful and angry, because our own needs are not being met.

<u>Mother</u>

Mother by name and Mother by nature
This earth has been Man's for the Eons of Time
But not any more will I take up my cross
For I have borne it too long and it's time to let go
And be ME – VALERIE

-o-o-0-o-o-

BE STILL

Be still, nature whispers
Be still and <u>know.</u>
Be still – that's what you must always do first.
Then the 'Being' part of you can come out to play and inspire and inform the 'doing' part of you.

And being still, what do we know?

That we do not have to <u>give</u> love,
For we <u>are</u> love …
we do not have to <u>seek</u> joy,
for we <u>are</u> joy,
we do not have to <u>make</u> peace
for we <u>are</u> peace.

Being these things, they spread out from us quite naturally, and go where they are needed.
Remaining still, we can move the whole world.

-o-0-o-

FROM WORRY TO CARE FREENESS

In 7 easy steps.

1. Listen to God. Have Faith in Him
2. Do what he tells you
3. Don't look back
4. Be true to yourself and what you believe
5. Let go of worries, give them to Him
6. Just show up, do your bit, move on
7. Leave all details to HIM, he does not need your help – then live every day.

And all your Energy will be returned in full for what you want to do for you.

This is the True Nature of us all.

-o-o-0-o-o-

What is Love – Love is TIME

Love is listening and Giving and Sharing
Not taking and pushing and shoving
Love is Kind, Love is Gentle, Love is Peace
Not owning and controlling and demanding
Love is Freedom and Acceptance and Committing
Not belittling and begrudging and restricting.

Love is Time for oneself and each other
Love is Bending and Humbling and Respecting
<u>Not</u> dominating and ruling and abusing
The Gentle Soul of Another

LOVE IS POWER.

Anything else is FEAR.

My Time and My Love are the most precious gifts I can give to a hungry world.

NO MORE PAIN! The end of Grief

No more pain, no more sadness
It's time to let go of the life that <u>was</u> ours
The tears, the regrets, the losses we've had
Are all in the past and there must remain
If we are all to be <u>happy and live</u> once again

This new life we've made will not be the same
But richer, and stronger, more vital than ever
For our children need us in the NOW not the past
They deserve our attention, so they don't know GUILT
For that's what keeps us stuck
It's the glue that won't let us open our hearts
To ourselves once again and each other.

So let the forgiveness begin and the anger dissolve
There's good times ahead and riches beyond
the material world
Remember the good and there was <u>so much</u>

But stay focused in today
For it's all we have and each day
Is special simply because we are here
To see each new experience and feel
The love that is there for us all from the Source

So let the Healing begin for the freedom <u>is</u> there
Inside each one of us, inside our hearts
And <u>we</u> hold the key that can lock or unlock
The Peace of Mind, the Joy and the Love
That we were born with, our birthright from God
Let's claim it now, put down the pain
And pick up the Love instead.

PAIN

… The Call of the Soul

Pain, oh Blessed Pain
I do not push you away any more
But listen to your call
Your call to stop and go within
For that is where the Pain began

I listen carefully now to you
And thank you for showing me the Truth
The way to be
The way to go
And the way back home to God.

When I didn't listen
It just got worse
And the louder it became
In my Soul's desperate attempt to
Get my attention again.

And when I give you
My full attention
And listen to the pleas
The pain recedes and
I can proceed with my Life
And my journey again in Peace

(Red)   Stop and Be Still

(Amber)   Go within and Ask, then <u>listen</u>!

(Green)   Get on with your journey in Truth and Peace

-o-o-0-o-o-

Stop and be still

Go within and Ask, then <u>listen</u>!

Get on with your journey
in Truth and Peace

To My Family

What Your Love Means to Me

It means my Life has had a purpose
For in giving life to you
You have given me so much to store
As treasure in my heart to share with others
Every day my life means so much more.

You have each and every one taught me more than you'll ever know
And for ever I'll be grateful to God
For giving me a 'Soul Mate' and together we produced
Three Special Beings full of Light and of Love
And they in turn have found their Mates
And given me 'oh' so much, much more
Than I ever thought could possibly be
And the learning still goes on for they are great teachers too
And I'm a willing student to them
Will I ever earn a degree!!

Yes I feel that I have – no cap and gown required
No bit of paper, or special ceremony
The degree I've earned is in <u>LOVE</u> and <u>RESPECT</u>
And for this there's no prize needed
No shouts or clapping required for
"I AM" LOVE

-o-o-0-o-o-

PEACE

Tonight there's a peaceful feeling in me which seems to have crept up on me without my realising it was there.

There is no-one to blame any more
I am seeing through the eyes of an adult now and not that small child in me.

I understand
I feel so calm, so empowered, knowing that I am in total control of my life and have let go of so much.

This is a feeling I have never experienced in my life before, one of calm composure and love.

My heart feels open and free, I do not care anymore how I look, how I seem to the world.

I am ready to let go of the past that has cursed me so long and so hard. I have even lost my craving for sweet things too, I am not hungry, not scared, not anything anymore, but this peaceful space inside is growing and expanding and my <u>knowing</u> is strong – I am THERE, no more WAITING, no more struggling, I can just be ME.

I am ok. I am Brilliant. I am Wonderful. I am Magnificent. I am free as a Bird to soar Higher and Higher and more Powerful than ever before. Look out world here I come with my message from my Creator.

Speak the Truth, be Yourself, never care what They might say or do.

Just get on with it, Life's Here now, just speak up, enjoy it, celebration time is here and I share it with You, my Family, my Friends, my helpers seen and unseen, and all of creation.

I am actually Seeing for the first time the amount of work and dedication I have had for my own healing and putting my beliefs into practice.

I am proud of my achievements so far and know I have more and more potential within me to explore now I am free of the past.

Believe me it is worth it, however long it takes, to have this feeling.

A big THANK You to my Family and all my Supporters and Helpers.

-o-o-0-o-o-

PERFECTION

The Dictionary says:
State of Being Perfect.
Complete, finished, whole, unspoilt, faultless,
correct, precise, excellent,
of Highest Quality.

What right have you, what right have I
To deny that this is so?
It's our true nature to 'BE'
Not '<u>TO DO</u>' not '<u>TO TRY</u>'
To improve, but just '<u>to grow</u>.'

We are planted here in this place we call earth
And given a chance to live and survive
To experience all, open up and receive
Then give back what we have learned
What have I learned? You may well ask
And I will tell you this

The more I live the more I know
The more I listen the more I grow
The more I share the more I have
The more I'm willing the longer I live

I'll tell you why if you care to listen
There really is nothing to 'DO'
For if I'm just willing then God does the rest
And he does it through me not BY ME
So no effort is involved

With no effort it's not work
But pure joy and pure love

To just give to each other
And receive it all back

This is nature at its best
That it can possibly be
Being born, being alive, being ME

And when I have finished this journey of mine
I'll lay down the body my Spirit calls home
And return to God with my story to be told
Of the earth and my life and how it was for me

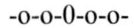

-o-o-0-o-o-

POVERTY CONSCIOUSNESS

What is the most precious gift that we can give to anyone else?

TIME AND LOVE

This is my gift I give to the world for it is
What there is Never Enough of

You have to make time to <u>be</u> together and
Listen, to talk, to love, because that is
What makes a happy family or team.

With a happy team you will be an enormous
Magnet of energy, which will automatically
Draw business and other people towards you
Without doing anything.

BEING is the hardest thing to be, but we
Are Human Beings not Human Doings and when you just BE yourselves people will source you out, they will give to you without you even trying to find them. In fact everything you <u>need</u> just shows up when you need it. This is the Magic of Life, pure synchronicity.

Lighten up you are all far too serious.
It is not about Money, it is about Life and Living and Happiness. It is impossible not to draw people to you when you are HAPPY

-o-o-0-o-o-

POWER

At last it is here, this belonging I have to something more Powerful than life itself.

To know I have this within my grasp and it is real and magical.

I own my power and I am free to be who I want to be.

I shine my light for all to see and let them know the Power is ME!

I am not just a channel, but know I am much more and now acknowledge it is so.

Gone are my Fears now my power is back and no longer will I hide it away.

-o-o-0-o-o-

PROCESS (2)

The process of Life is a Simple One
If only we let it be so
It's feeling the pain that everyone shares
Then dealing only with your own.

When we interfere in someone else's pain
We are slowing their process down
For they alone have to deal with it all
To return to the Love of God.

Which is there all the time
But is not allowed into their hearts
So cold to themselves
So listen they must to the call from within
And make their journey back to where they began.

The feelings we dislike are the ones that teach us most
About what is going on in our hearts
So feel them we must, own them only as our own
Speak to someone who cares and can hold your heart
While you struggle to let go of the hurt

A friend who will judge not, all the feelings you feel
As you come to terms with yourself
Not one who will use and abuse your Trust

Learn <u>discernment</u> and then just be REAL
For that's what is needed more than anything now
In this world full of judgments and scorn
To be Real is God's call to us all
And Authentic above everything else!

No more pretending and not being ourselves
For dishonesty destroys our soul.

-o-o-0-o-o-

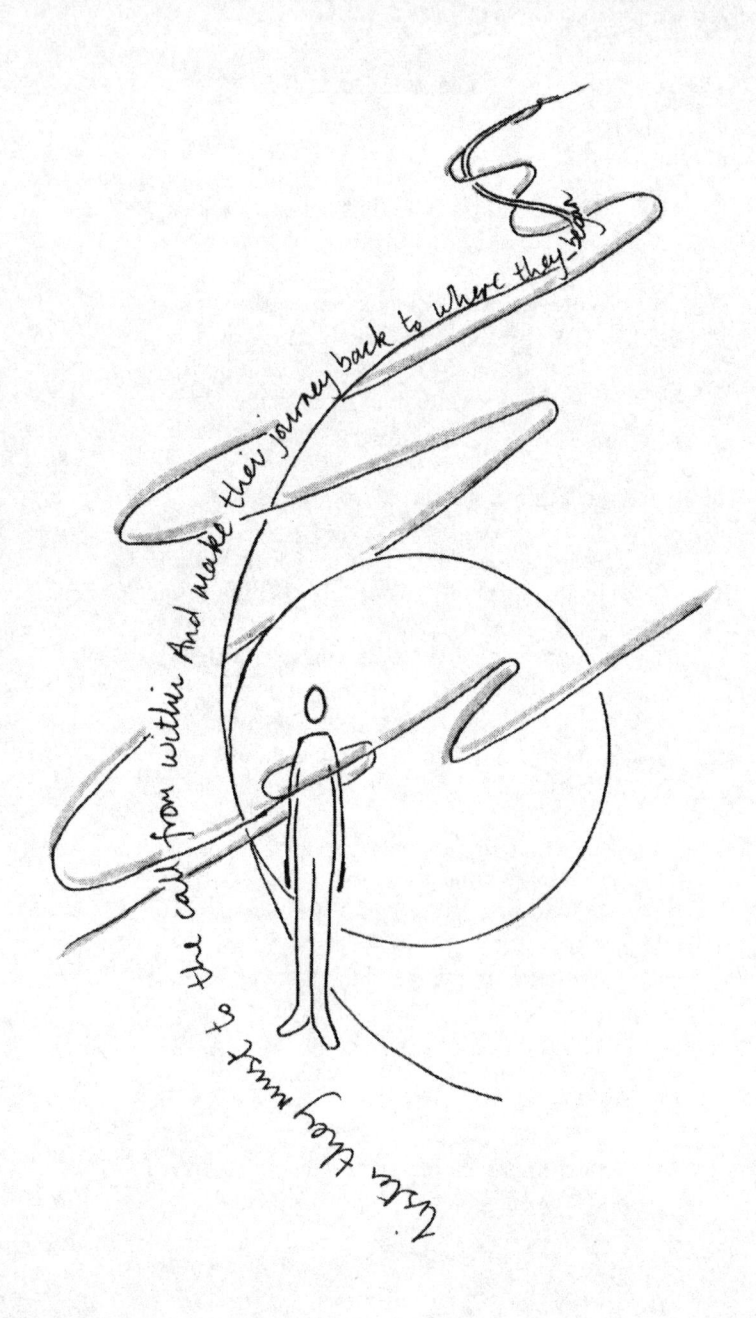

Until they must to the call from within And make their journey back to where they began

Letting off Steam and BEING ME

Pressures from within I PUT ON MYSELF

To help everyone
To enjoy life
To be out there in the world doing
To be having fun
To be Doing Something
To making it happen
To Being with friends
To feel good all the time
To cope well all the time
To not show it if I am upset
To get it Right
To be all things to all people
To understand it all
To learn more
To grow more
To Give
To Receive
To let Go
To HELP
And even to BE

WHY

TO BE RECOGNISED!

It was great and right at the time.
THAT IS A HELL OF A LOT OF PRESSURE!

-o-o-0-o-o-

THE PRESSURE COOKER – Time and Energy

What a wonderful thing the pressure cooker was
To save Time and Energy
Or so we thought
But the feeling now is a different tale
For we realise that life is just fraught
With this very same need
And we are ready to burst
For the pressure's too high
And what is inside just has to come out
With a sigh and a wail!!
We let it all go
And now the slow Cooker is all the go

For the Time and Energy is not well spent
When we hold it all in
With no other vent
And the only way out is to take off the lid
And look inside at what we have made
Is it good, is it edible, or is it just mush!
Let us start again and do it real slow
And enjoy the process, however long
And the smell of the cooking and Life as it is
No more rushing and pushing to save
Our Time and our Energy
Where did it all go!!
Was it wasted? OH NO!

-o-o-0-o-o-

Questions to ask within yourself

What do I believe about

My Life
My Purpose
My Body
My Relationships
My Work
My Health
Men
Women
Religion

Who taught me these?

Do I need to hold on or release these?

My Beliefs will always create my Reality no matter what I decide to do with MY MIND – self sabotage.

If we don't have unlimiting and supportive Beliefs, then we can never achieve what we really want.

-o-o-0-o-o-

<u>Satisfaction</u>

Through the eyes of my soul
I look back at my Life
And it's pleased I am with Myself
And what I've achieved through the struggle and pain
And the Trust I have found again
With God's gentle hands and my Angels to care

I've been '<u>carried</u>' and '<u>pushed</u>' along
On this journey called Life
This experience of Love
Which embraces it all as a whole

And the oneness I feel consumes all the pain
And the heartache that's felt by us all
For the suffering souls that are burning in Hell
Not out there, but "<u>within</u>" themselves.

For you see that the peace and the love lies within
And the '<u>Heaven</u>' your heart desires
But you have to come through all the struggle and strife
To get to the other side

But the Light is so bright
If you follow its beam
And tread where others have trod
And the hands reach out to
love and support you
on your way through
What I call the <u>Tunnel of Love</u>
For although it is dark

The end is always in sight
So all you have to do
Is to turn on your Light, use the Power within
And listen, you will be guided through
There <u>is only one way</u> and
That's through God.

So I'm satisfied with my life
And what I've achieved for me
This book tells it all so you may <u>know</u>
Pick up your 'phone and dial to God

HIS DIRECT LINE IS ALWAYS FREE!

No need to wait for a line to be clear
Or an operator to intervene
No need to hold on, you'll not be cut off
Speak clearly and give your problems to God

Then wait for an answer to be given
Stay listening and open, the answers will come
Via his many channels on earth
Someone's voice, a feeling, a meeting, a friend
Or by nature as you wait, it will be revealed

The signs and the symbols are always there
When you're ready to listen and Trust
So stop <u>your Control</u> and trying to organise it all
Let it be all done for you

Then the living it all and the loving it all

Is God as he uses you and no more
Will you 'WORK' when you find your true self
For God does it all through you
NOT BY YOU

So no effort's involved, no more struggle and pain
JUST BEING as he intended you to be
No more battle within, no more enemies 'out there'
Just Peace for us all as it was intended to be

Heaven on Earth we'll proclaim
With a shout full of Joy
Is the future we're promised
And we're a part of it all

What an awesome privilege to be here on Earth at this great time of change!!

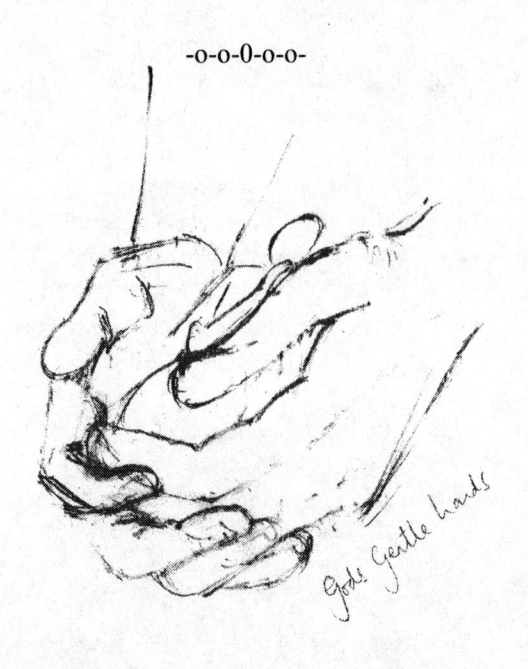

-o-o-0-o-o-

Gods Gentle hands

OVERWHELMED

This feeling comes and goes
I can't always take it in
What God wants to give me is so much
It scares me the enormity of it all.

So I back off once again and tell myself
I'm not ready to receive it all
It's so awesome, immense and amazing
Like nothing on earth I've experienced before

What is it – you ask – that scares me so
It's a feeling I cannot describe
Except to say it's like walking into a huge, huge store
And being told at the doors – "it's all yours."

"It's yours for the taking
It's yours to explore
It's yours to enjoy and experiment with"
So why – you may ask – do I not grab it all?
Why do I stand here and just gaze in AWE?

The real reason is – you see – I feel I'm so small
In comparison with God and the world
I can't handle it, or so my Fear tells me
And I argue with God once again
As he tells me, "Wake up to the world
It's all yours – I want you to have it all"

And enjoy your new life – it's what you've <u>awaited</u>
Open your eyes, let go of the smallness within
Wake up to your Greatness and then you can begin

TO LIVE IN HEAVEN ON EARTH

<u>The choice is YOURS</u>

THROUGH MY body God has shown me who I am, through the aches and pains, through my size I now RECOGNISE GOD.

My body manifests itself as bigger and larger than ever before until I recognise my Greatness, my True Greatness that is shared by all.

I make the choice to wake up, rub the sleep from my eyes, stretch my limbs, feel my weight in the world I've created for myself. I stand tall and am ready to be counted by God, who wants this new Message for us all. <u>I</u> made you to be <u>Great</u> each and every one of you, so listen to the message Valerie's words convey.

Be inspired, be alive and stop waiting around. Take your chance in the world and accept all I give you. It is what you came here for.

You are created in my image of True Greatness:

The "I AM"

And my purpose is just TO BE ME.

Thank you God from my heart within your heart.

Wake up and remember – it's simple you see – there's nothing to learn for you already know.

-o-o-0-o-o-

The Simple pleasures in life for me are –

Sitting in my chair silently and looking out into my beautiful garden

Being with my grandchildren and just observing them and their simplicity

Being with friends, talking and listening and sharing opinions openly and honestly

Seeing the pleasure on someone's face when they recognise who they are

Being in nature

People watching

Observing the Games people play, pure entertainment

-o-o-0-o-o-

SWEET SORROW

Is just what might have been
Our hopes, our plans, our dreams
But they just slip by unnoticed by us
'til we realise it's too late

But the secret is, there are many more
We can substitute if we wish
So let go of 'what if's' and 'if only's'
Move on into Bliss and the promise
Of good things to come

Let the world take over and receive what comes
With a heart wide open and arms ready to receive
For life is what happens, when you just let go
And be in this moment and are just glad to be alive?

And able to see and feel and hear
And experience all and embrace it all
For this is it – there's nowhere to go
And nothing to be striving for

This is Love, this is Life, this is Peace
And I thank God for showing me the way
To Bliss and transcending this body of mine
For I have arrived and accepted it all
This is wholeness, this is my true nature
JUST BEING ME

-o-o-0-o-o-

Be still and Listen to the Call of the Soul

"Be still" my Soul keeps telling me
"Be still and be at Peace"
But my mind keeps wanting me to do something
Anything, I am flitting from one thing to the next

"Stop and listen", the voice says
"Take it in, all around you there I am
You are not hearing me".

Stop and listen to the sounds
To the buzz of excitement as the world carries on
The birds are singing, the breeze is blowing gently on my face
Someone is sawing wood, children's laughter, in the distance
voices
Cars are moving and behind it all I hear God laughing
At me because I cannot take it in
At me because I want to miss it all
THIS <u>IS</u> LIFE!
A dog is barking, flies are buzzing
Never ceasing noise, but comforting nevertheless
Children playing, adults working
And where am I in all of this
<u>Where am I</u>?

You are all of it – it is you
But I don't feel it today
I have lost my connection it seems
And immediately the pressure is there in my head
I am trying too hard TO BE just like
I tried too hard to <u>do</u>
For fear of getting it wrong
"Just let go and Surrender", God says,
"Surrender to your heart, live in love not the fear
for your heart is ME and I AM YOU
be still and notice" – just notice.

-o-o-0-o-o-

"Be Still" my soul keeps telling me
"Be Still and be at Peace"

GAZING AND DREAMING – An Extension of Time

How I have missed this process in Life
Of standing and staring and seeing into the beyond
As a child I was good at this creating my own world
Making things happen as I wanted them to do
But somewhere between then and now it got lost
Along the way in the process we call life
Now I have discovered it again and
The mystery is once more revealed
For the Key is in my Heart and my Desire is strong
For my spirit of adventure is reborn
My Heart strings are pulling and calling me home
To the land I once knew in my dreams
Now can I remember, is it all coming back
Yes be patient and listen my heart says

BE STILL!

-o-o-0-o-o-

STAYING STRONG

When all around you is collapsing in FEAR

Stay with yourself, your vision, your HOPE.

Listen inside, take your time and just wait

For the moment will come when the TRUTH is revealed

Your Strength is your Power and so is your LOVE

For those who are weakened by Life and its cares

The Fear loses power when confronted by LOVE

For the Fear is not Truth and the Fear is not REAL

It is all an
ILLUSION -
ONLY LOVE IS REAL

Let Love Light the Way.

-o-o-0-o-o-

<u>Who am I?</u>

Who am I? I am the Soul, the Light Divine
And I will shine my Light today
For all to see and guide them on their way
Back to who they are and why they're here
And what Life's about.

It's a wonderful life if only we could be
Ourselves and not who we are expected to be.

Where did it all go wrong?
Why has it all been lost?
That mutual respect between Men and Women
For the differences we have
And the help we can be to each other
If only we could see.

What is there to see? I ask myself
Beneath the layers of time
We are so vulnerable it seems
In this physical body we have chosen.

But I am much more than this body of mine
And I will reach such heights
Never reached before
Because I <u>choose</u> to <u>LIVE</u> my life
And be guided from within, not out there any more

So come, my soul, and teach me how
To transcend this body of mine
And live the Life I'm intended to live
One of Love, Joy and Peace and the Divine.

-o-o-0-o-o-

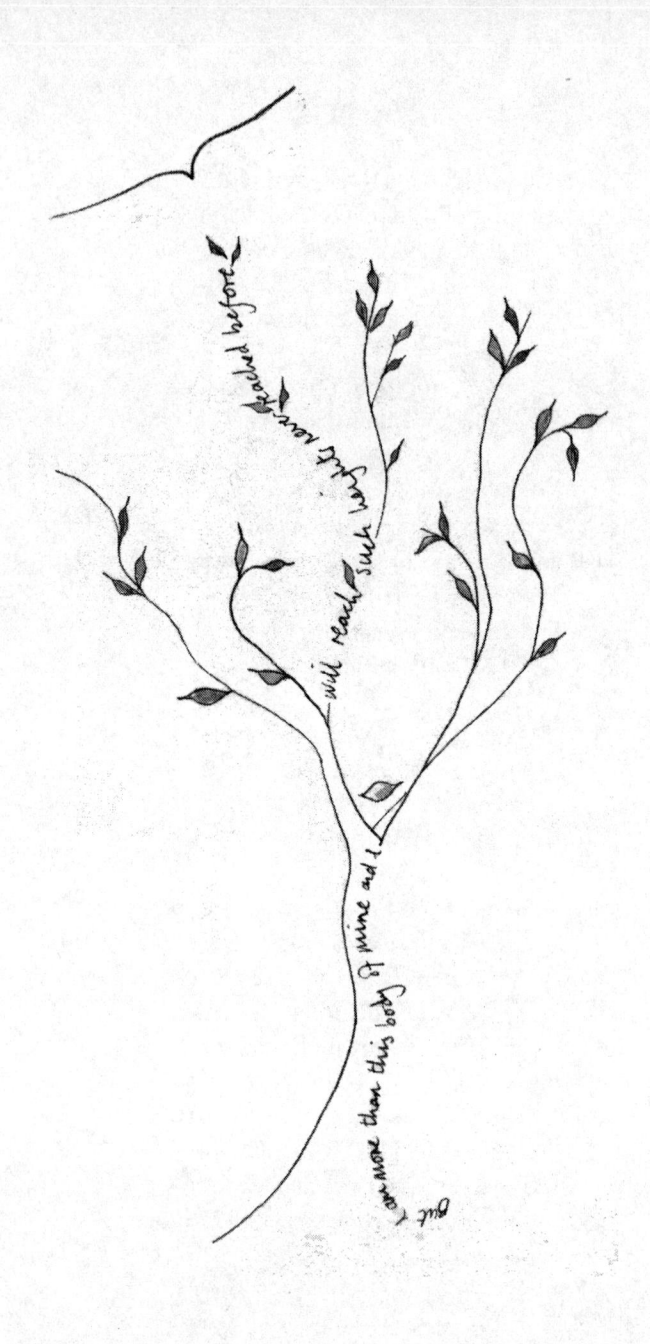

But I am more than this body of mine and I will reach such heights unimagined before.

EYES WIDE OPEN

With eyes wide open I now can see
What love is really about
Not having or getting or making or doing
But <u>Being</u> and <u>Sharing</u> and <u>Seeing</u> and <u>Loving</u>

When we are low in spirit, we do not see
What Life is giving to us
We live in the Fear of losing it all
It is such a material world.

But what I now know is my Needs have been met
By God who always provides
My heart is wide open, my arms fully stretched
To receive all He gives me Inside.

And what I have inside is Joy, Love and Peace
My Strength is second to none
So now I see through the Eyes of Love
What Life is really about.

Life is for Living and Being <u>not</u> Doing
For Shining and Spreading the Light
So that others might see in the Way that I see
Through the Eyes of LOVE not FEAR! Or DOUBT!

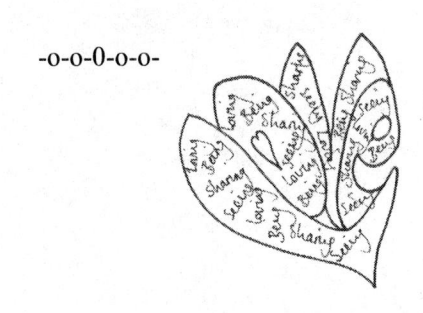

-o-o-0-o-o-

A Cold March Day – Home is where my Heart is

The winds may howl
And the winds may blow
But inside me is a wonderful glow
From my Inner Sun that shines so bright
And lights my path back to God/Love

This feeling inside is one of pure bliss
And my Love extends far and wide
From the depth of my Being
My Soul cries out
This is Love, this is You, this is God.

I have reached it at last
My journey complete
This is what I came to the Earth for
To experience Love in its many forms
And to teach what this Love is for

The journey was hard and at times I just felt
I couldn't go on any more
But just when my hopes reached their lowest point
God would lift me again as before
When I asked him for help
He was always around and listening to my sighs and my woes
Ever patient, ever loving, ever consoling my mind
And waiting for me to let go
And surrender my Will and let him take the strain
And the pain and the guilt and the work
For when I let go he takes over my Life
And all is well and happy once more.
In the Flow

-o-o-0-o-o-

*for when I let go
he takes over my life*

*and all is happy
once more in the flow*

Nobody Hears Me

I hear them all cry
No-one is listening to ME
But the Truth is revealed and the hurting exposed
To the Light, when it all explodes

And they see that the pain they are
Carrying is shared by them all
So scream on and let it all go
For until the screaming dies down

Then the listening cannot begin
And in the listening we find a way
Back to the Truth and ourselves
For the energy has gone to keep fighting within
And hurting ourselves with the Pain

Forgiving comes next and acceptance the key
So the love can all flow once more
To restore to the whole with no conditions attached
The illusion all shattered, the True Picture Revealed

There's no separation at all
Love is all.

-o-o-0-o-o-

The Power of Love and Forgiveness

Forgiveness comes when the barriers are down and all is then revealed …
When the secrets hidden long before can surface to be healed.
For the loss of childhood then we grieve and our life as it should have been
With two parents who were victims of society and the past
Of what went on behind closed doors in a world full of dark and fear

But the roles played out were beyond control of my mother now so dear
And time will heal these open wounds which now have been exposed
By the light of God will true love reveal all that should have been.

For two souls united once again in the light of what went on
My mum and I will shed some tears, but our hearts will now be whole
And our eyes will see anew what life can really hold
When our faith in God has been fulfilled and our stories both are told
To those who need to hear how life cruelly treated us both by a man, who has wronged us all in his lonely search for love –

And the sadness is that he too was wronged in his life upon this earth
So that in the end there's no-one to blame, let us just be glad that for us this is past and perhaps we can now move on and forgive and forget
For, if we don't, it has all been in vain, my struggle and my pain
For release for us both in this world of sin
To reclaim our life and reach out again in hope and peace and joy

Many lives will be healed when we forgive and that is a Promise from God.

So if we can help others on the way, then our mission will not be a total waste and we can all hold our heads up once again and say we are proud of ourselves.

We deserve all now that life can hold and the Universe will provide for all our needs in many ways,
Just Trust, have faith and be healed.

Let your anger dissolve in the love and the light for it truly will destroy all that you hold dear
And the future generations will be proud to call us their own
For we are unique and that's a fact that is true
To have healed and stopped this abuse of life
And Respect is all we can now expect.

-o-o-0-o-o-

The Big Lie – The Illusion

Now I know who "I am" and the secret is out
I can reveal the Lie I have been telling myself
That I was separate from God and the rest of the world
And in fact I was terribly <u>small</u>!

In my Mind I created a story of me
And that story has now been told
But that's all it was, just a story you see
And not the Real Me at all.

For the Real Me you see before you now
Is who I came to BE
And all the rest was just false and a role I played out
On the stage of life – don't you SEE?

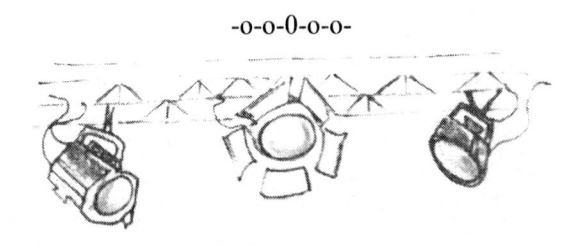

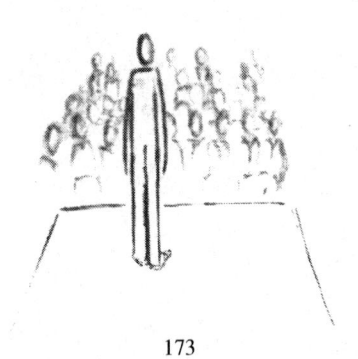

-o-o-0-o-o-

Opposites

How do you recognise yourself and who you are if you do not experience everything that you <u>are not</u>?
I now OWN my Greatness
Let it now be revealed
For I will not hide myself any more
No more Games, no more Roles
Will I play in this world
Only "Mine" the Creator of it all.

So ready I am to move into my Light
And be all I came to be
For at the end of it all
Is the beginning of it all
And that is how it's meant to be.

INFINITY

-o-o-0-o-o-

Through the Eyes of a Child

Give me something simple
A bucket and spade
Some soil, some sand or some water
And I will show you the pleasures of life
In my little world that <u>I see</u>

Not the great big world that you all get involved in
<u>My</u> world is <u>as small as can be</u>
But if everyone kept to their bit of this place
What a happier World it would be!

-o-o-0-o-o-

A letter to MY 'SELF' from 'MY' HOLY SPIRIT

To see you as I see you
Is to know you as I know you
To love you as I love you
Is to love everyone the same

Your heart is wide open
Your petals unfurled
Your scent is as sweet as can be
You bloom briefly to die
So you can bloom again and again
Each bloom as perfect as the last
Each stem fed by my love.

As you expose your True Self
To the world that you see
They will know and believe what you say
For your way is 'The Way', 'The Truth' and the Life
Nothing more, nothing less ALL LOVE

-o-o-0-o-o-

Where am "I" now?

Where am "I" now
What is it all about
This Life I have come to live
My mind is clear
My Soul is free
My Heart is in Eternity

But where am "I", I ask My "Self"
Not here, not there, not anywhere
It seems to be the strangest quest
That I'm about on Earth

Have I let go, am I holding on
Am I there, am I here
Am I all around
I keep searching it seems, but the answer is here
Right under my nose it would seem

So if I stop looking, maybe then I will know
The answer to my quest
Is it me, is it you, is it God – I don't know
Yes you do, yes you do of, course it is God

What else is there to be
What else would you want
To be All of it through and through
Round and round, no need to look
No need to see, you are Me, I am You
We are all there is to be LOVE

-o-o-0-o-o-

My Life

I feel like a flower that has just unfurled
My petals wide for all to see
There is no shame or innocence there
Just the Very Core of Me.

My stem is strong and woody now
Where once it was small and thin
My heart is open, my Love is strong
The Dear Lord Enters in.

-o-o-0-o-o-

Wake-up! Wake-up!

Is the message coming through
Are you seeing are you hearing
<u>Who</u> is coming through?

Are you still waiting
Are you praying
Has your message been received?

Do you linger on the threshold
Is your body now restored
Are you sure? Are you ready?

What are you waiting for?

Your life's your own
To do with as <u>you</u> will
It has been all along

You've taken it and moulded it
Examined it and constructed your own theory
Now look at it again through your new Eyes
Look at your Life – look at your Love

Be at Peace with it all

For it's Perfect and wonderful
Amazingly believable
The illusion has gone and you are free
Always have been, always will be <u>ME.</u>

-o-o-0-o-o-

Standing straight and tall, like the Old Oak Tree

When I stand tall and straight like the Old Oak Tree
I shelter you from the storms of life
When I am weighed down and my branches hang low
You cannot see me at all.

For many years I have leaned on one and another
For fear of being Myself
But now I know where my Energy went
For it has suddenly all returned.

If I lean on you, my weight <u>you</u> feel
If <u>you</u> lean on me, it is a burden I cannot carry
There is only one way to be I have learned
To stand in the Truth and the Love and the Light

My branches now go towards the Light
As I extend and put out new Growth
My roots go deep into my Mother – the Earth
And her nourishment now I feel.

Connected I am to the Earth and the Light
One foot in Heaven, one below
My Soul sings with Joy now that I have returned
Full circle at last, I have PEACE!

I celebrate Life and all that it brings
So freely to my door
It has always been there, but my eyes open wide
To see what Beauty is "in store".

-o-o-0-o-o-

Archangel Michael

This is a Message from Michael the Great

It is one of Peace and Love and Success for the world if, we listen to the messages that are being given out. These messages contain the secret of Life. They are meant only for those people who want to be happy and spread that happiness wherever they go.

These messages are not for the fainthearted and those who are selfish and greedy – they are for the Selfless Ones.

My first message comes to give you a Promise from God, that you will be taken care of and provided for in every way, if you follow his Path of Love and Truth.

My second message is that we are called upon to give ourselves now in Service to our Maker. This service will give you all you need for your own lives, in order to show others what can be achieved. This will be termed as Heaven on Earth or Heaven within yourself.

My next message comes from the Heart of the World, which is broken and hurt and needs repair. You are all to help in this Healing of the Planet on which you live. So much has been destroyed and if you do not do something soon it will be too late. You have to wake up to your purpose and Who you Are, you do not have long to do this!!

Those who are committed to this work will be Rich beyond measure and will be happier than they ever thought possible, but you have to do your own inner work and "walk your talk" as you say on Earth.

It is no good preaching to others if you do not commit your own Time and Love to yourself.

The only way is to SHOW PEOPLE, not teach them how to do it.

My last message is for those of you who are not on this path, your work will <u>not</u> be successful, you will have problem after problem if you are solely for your <u>own</u> needs and your <u>own</u> success. The choice is yours.

God HAS SPOKEN!

-o-o-0-o-o-

BLISS

The Secret of Happiness is to let go of all <u>my</u> thoughts and I am happy.

I feel light and free in my heart, free to be who <u>I</u> want to be, Say what I want. I accept myself as I am. I celebrate who I am, what I am and why I'm here.
I know my True Purpose in Life and that is to be happy, to be <u>ME</u> and let go of everything. I hand the Controls over to my Creator and set myself free.

This is a truly wonderful feeling.

Nothing and no-one has any POWER or CONTROL over me.

This is Bliss!

-o-o-0-o-o-

My Dearest One

My Angels:
You have reached the end of your journey 'on Earth', so why are you worrying about making more changes? Just let go now and let God give you all.

Me:
What do you mean by my journey on Earth? Does that mean I am going back to God and leaving my body?

Angels:
No dear one – it means you will be in Heaven on Earth and show others the way, but in order to do that you must let go and just be, so that God can give you the Miracle of Transformation. Do you understand?

Me:
Yes, the journey on Earth then, is that what we think of as Hell on Earth?

Angels:
Yes, I'm afraid it is because that is what 'Man' has turned it into in his mind.

If you let go all will be revealed and you will be at complete Peace. It is not your time. You will decide that, no-one else!

Me:
Is that in my control then (as I've always believed it to be?) that I decide when I will die and go home?

Angels:
Yes of course it is with EVERYONE!

-o-o-0-o-o-

To be an Angel

Christine

Thank you for being my Friend
Thank you for being there
Thank you for your simplicity
Thank you for being YOU

Thank you for your Loyalty
Thank you for your ability to be Real
Thank you for your Unique way of being
Thank you for your Laughter

You add Light to My Life

I send you my Light and My Love.

-o-o-0-o-o-

What I see Clearly Now

You can read me like an open book. I'm Transparent.

What I see clearly now is me a creator of all I see in <u>my</u> world
And it's beautiful and awesome this creation of mine
For all I see is ME.

My world is so full of beautiful things
To feast my eyes upon
And life is so wondrous and marvellous and bright
Pure Beauty and Goodness in it all.

And my heart goes out to you as you read
My thoughts I share with you all
For 'I am' the book, and the living it was good
So I leave it open now for you all to read.

And I live wide open so you too can see
In me what your life is about
It's about You, no-one else, for don't you see
You too are the author like me

So Title your Book and live to its cover
And its words, be honest and true to yourself
Be transparent and clear, be as Real as can be
For this is the Authentic You you were created to be
Made in God's Image – Perfection at its Best

This is MY WORK, it's what I came to do
To finally find my Truth
And the Kingdom of Heaven both within and without
Of myself

Just Believe in Myself and trust in Myself, then all my dreams will
come true.

So from this day hence I make a vow
And a strong commitment to me
Live only for NOW leave the rest to God
Think the thoughts send them out
And wait for the Creation to come to me.

I want it all I want it now I'm ready to receive the
Love
Peace
Joy
Trust
Comfort
Kindness
Gentleness
Stillness
Healing
Beauty
Serenity

… The Miracles of Life and Living

for you are the creator of all you see
so if you aren't happy with 'yourself'
start again, and create in your thoughts and your heart
how you think and feel it should be.

For the choice is yours and your screen is clear
It's your world again don't you see
Put in it your light and the players you want
Create your way for that's the way it should be.
YOUR CREATION – YOUR WORLD
What you want for YOURSELF.

So I begin at the beginning and put in my world
The people I want to see
The people who love me for what I am

And support me in all I do
The ones who are happy and loving their life
And creating like me, what 'they' want to see
Let the rest pass me by with never a look
Only beauty and love will exist in my world
As I look in the mirror and the reflection looks at me
It will see!

My Soul aches, my heart aches, for me to return
And be at one with myself
My body cries out in its longing for love
To be restored to the Masterpiece of God
As I welcome Him back fully in my life once more
I can begin once again in Hope and Joy
And my Energy is fully restored
In the Love and the Light and the Miracle of Grace

No more roles will I play for I will create
I will direct I will conduct it all
For my Destiny is mine and I will use it well
This 'CHOICE' God has given "ME ALL"

WOW!

OH GOD. I LOVE YOU AND YOU LOVE ME THAT IS ALL I NEED FOR ETERNITY

-o-o-0-o-o-

WHAT NOW?

What now, I ask, now the secret's revealed
And I can create the life I choose
I know all the ways my life did not work
So there's only one option now to see

That 'I am' the source of all I see
And all I see is Me
And the Best of it all <u>is the Truth</u> of it all
Why would I settle for less
When God wants only the Best
So that is what I will choose
And let go of the rest

For I have the Power
And use it I will
To create only the best for me
And if others so choose, they can do the same
For they are no different from me.

So let's not pretend you are anything less
Than Magnificent, Awesome and Great
For this is our Birthright and claim it we must
Or surrender ourselves to the fate

That we are nothing but dust
With no Power at all
And in the Hands of the world out there
For this is not the case, so hurry up and wake up
To your 'Life' and the Living <u>IS GOOD</u>.

Mistakes are the mechanics by which we learn
What we <u>do not</u> want to <u>experience</u> again.
When we've tried all the 'so called wrong' ways
There's only one Way left and
That is the Right way for us.

The journey to self discovery means my Inner world now becomes my outer world, wonderful peace and harmony, excellent relationships and love wherever I go.

When you function in Love your inside creates your outside world
When you function in Fear your outside world creates your inside

Mechizadek

-o-o-0-o-o-

LOVE YOUR CHILDREN FOR WHO THEY ARE NOT WHAT THEY DO

Your children are special, they have lives of their own
And your role is clear, there is nothing <u>to do</u>
Except show them <u>love</u> and above all <u>respect</u>
Show them Truth, show them Strength and the Beauty within
Each and every one, point it out, make it clear
So there is no doubt that Beauty is Light
It is uniqueness and the qualities therein that we need
Not the Falseness, not the Pretence, not the glamour we see
But the realness, the gifts that we bring
To one another that are important and needed
By us all as we enter our New World within
Take off your masks, let them see you
For who you are, tell the truth
Be Real not Role Models telling them
This is what you should be
This is what you must do
Then going another way yourself
Showing them confusion of self
When you respond to your heart and its urgings you feel
And let go of the Fear in your head
Your children respond in a wonderful way
Not following others, being led astray
They'll remain true to themselves
And their innocence they will keep
Be a Shepherd, show them Wisdom
And take care of your Sheep
And as they grow up and follow your lead
Good shepherds they'll make for the poor and the weak
Who need someone to show them in times of great need
That it's from Example we learn, not the words that we Speak

-o-o-0-o-o-

A Mother's Words for my Sons and Daughter

Be at peace with your lives and the way you are choosing
For the outcome of it all will be
No more pain, no more hardship, no more fear, only love
That is my promise passed to me by God.

Love it all, resist it not, each new challenge you pursue
Will make you stronger and your purpose will be clear
To be yourself, authentic, real and true
No more falseness you pursue
No pretence, no more guilt only honesty will do
For this is freedom at its best and what <u>my</u> life is all about

And this is Love, no conditions attached, no more codes to undo
This is the Key to Life and Living your best
As you were intended to do
Seek only the Best for yourself
No limits, no "THIS WILL DO"
For this label tells the world you're <u>NOT GOOD ENOUGH</u>
And that's not what God wants for you.

-o-o-0-o-o-

MY TRIBUTE TO MUM

A life so hard, I just cannot conceive
How difficult and painful it was
To have lived through a war and the poverty it brought
And the scars left behind on the wounded souls

When the living was hard and the gains were few
With mouths to feed and many bodies to clothe
No 'help' then like today for the ones who were poor

When there was never enough of the things we have now
And no 'hand-outs' were around to ease them through
When all <u>she</u> wanted was a better life for her young
And all the things we take for granted now

But her life was not wasted or sacrificed in vain
For my happiness <u>is her</u> success
And a gift I can give her to show her why
Her part was an important role

For she taught me to take Responsibility for My Life
To be strong and detached from expecting my needs to be met
Through the family and to meet them myself

For she gave me a life and a chance to succeed
Where perhaps she feels she did not
And what she did then was not recognised
For that's how it was then
Women took a back seat and were often dismissed as
Just a mother
Just a housewife, that's all

So if she feels some regret, jealous feelings, bitterness and anger
for what she has missed
I will understand it all

For compassion and love is all there in my heart
And I give it back to her

So thank you Dear Mother – this comes from the heart
You are not responsible any more
For you have done your part
And the rest is up to me
To pass down the lessons you have taught

To be honest and True to myself first of all
And to heal myself from within
So our family tree will grow strong
And new growth will be seen
At the top of this Beautiful Tree.

I love you Mum.

-o-o-0-o-o-

Who am I? (2)

This question I asked myself
And this was the answer I received
From God who is my Friend,
And Creator of all things good

You are the Purest Light there ever could be
And you are here for all to see
Themselves in you as they should be
Happy and peaceful and free

Let them see you as you are
With no pretence and holding back
And you will be the greatest light on Earth
And Heaven will be your reward.

My child walk on towards the Light
And let <u>me</u> guide you home
For that is where your life will begin
And time on Earth became the Plan

For all to see and feel the love
Of God who loves them so
His children all have to return to him
When they remember who they are!

-o-o-0-o-o-

Why do we do too much

Because we don't feel valued as a Person

Because we feel Alone and Separate from God

We need to be LOVED and we don't feel loved in our Hearts, because we feel guilty, so we compensate by <u>doing</u> too much to pay off the guilt.

We don't get to feel LOVED 'til we Love ourselves fully and RESPECT ourselves for who and what we are.

If we <u>know</u> who we are and why we are here then the <u>need</u> in us for others to love us Disappears.

This does <u>not</u> mean that it's not wonderful to have someone love you, but just means that if they don't, you still feel happy and peaceful with yourself.

-o-o-0-o-o-

WORK!

This is the Price we Pay for Success

My loss is great, it is so hard to bear
This weight that I am feeling.
Time has moved on, but the weight remains
Dragging me down, making me Stop
To look and see what it's all about.

This "work" absorbs our very being
It hurts our Loving Soul
And pushes us further and further away
From the ones we love the most.

What is if for? I ask myself
What did it all begin?
When Man decided he had a Plan
To make his own success and Wealth

What is it that we are all looking for?
What have we lost along the way?
Our Peace of Mind, but more than that
OURSELVES as we should really be
HAPPY AND JOYFUL AND FREE

This sadness I feel overwhelms me so
That I can hardly see
The Truth of Life as it really should be
Instead of his legacy of pain

This is the result of one man's success
A family torn apart
At a time when we should be really close

And helping each other through with love and support
In our times of Need

But there is NOT TIME FOR LOVE
And the work demands its price
But the price tag's too high
And the loss is too great to bear.
Put it DOWN.

-o-o-0-o-o-

Written after my husband's death from a heart attack

-o-o-0-o-o-

TRY TO REMEMBER

"Try to remember" the song goes
but what is it we've forgotten
in our quest for life, we all seem to be
lost and alone, not sure where to turn
or who to follow
all trust is gone, only fear remains
in this world full of hate and despair
there is only one way out of this
hell we've created
and that is to follow our hearts

Does your body feel tired, no energy left
to do what you desire?
then listen my friend and go within
if you want your heart to sing again
ease off and listen before it's too late
and your heart gives up its pleas
"slow down" – it says, but you don't
hear it calling and pleading with you to stop.

"What are YOU DOING and WHY?" it says
Just stop and listen to ME
You were given a life to live my friend
Are you Living or is it "Pretend"
When will you wake up and realise you're stuck
In the illusion of Fear and the only
True Reality is LOVE

Stuck in the Mud

Stuck in Time and living in the past
He beats his drum wanting everyone to hear
It's not MY fault, it is all of you
Can't you hear me, can't you see me?
No, you only see yourselves, he thinks
But what he doesn't know is
He is Wrong and they are Right

But that won't do, "I am always Right"
He shouts and pouts like a spoilt child
"Grow up" God says, "grow up and fast
before you lose it all.

Grow up and be a Man at last
This is your Final Call.
Take up your cross and follow me
Take up your own Responsibility
For the life you create is the life you
Are living, and you have no Peace.

"It is My way or not at all" –
We hear him cry, if only he knew
His way was wrong, that is why he's lost
And cannot find his way back to himself.

-o-o-0-o-o-

Heart Attack!

Why does the Heart Attack
And show me all this scorn?
Why does it stop me in my tracks
And take away all I've striven for?

Why does it cause me all this Pain
And take away My Control?
Why does it end up scarred for life
And give me nothing in return?

Why should I stop, you may well ask.
What have I ever done wrong?
I have worked and worked my fingers to the bone
I have never been idle or sat around alone.

In my toil and strife for what I think is right
Why should I stop? But <u>stop</u> I must
For this heart just won't let me carry on
Be STILL it says, "be STILL"!

Be STILL and know yourself my Friend
Be STILL and listen to WHY
Your heart has stopped you in your tracks
And given you a chance <u>NOT</u> to die.

You are much too busy working, my friend
To listen to your heart of gold
You are much too busy to listen to God
And what he really wants for you.

God sent you here to learn, my friend
To experience love and joy and peace
But you have gone away from him
And decided <u>you</u> know what is best!
So you have worked your heart too hard

And not listened to its pleas:
"Take care of Me, look after Me
And show Me <u>love</u>", it screams to you.

But you attack yourself more and more
By pushing and shoving your body on
So your heart hits back at you and says:
"You <u>will listen, you will hear</u>", you have one more chance.
Get it right or just move on alone.

Your heart is for Giving and Loving my child
Firstly unto yourself
For until you can give to yourself, my friend
How can you give to anyone else?

God gives you Love in the Purest form
With no conditions attached
He gives you Life, he gives you JOY
The rest is up to you.

What do you get then in return
For giving this love to yourself?
You get to share it around, my friend
With those you love the most and those you
Have chosen to SHARE THIS LIFE WITH, YOU
BECOME THE GIFT TO THEM – YOUR TRUE SELF

-o-o-0-o-o-

"Survival of a Heart Attack"

"Why me?" I hear him cry, "why Me?"
to be stopped in my prime by this heart of mine
I am puzzled and perplexed by my pain
I have lived a good life as a good wholesome man
I have always done my best
I have prayed to God, I have given myself
To my work and My own life Plan

But what you don't know, my friend
Is that your little plan doesn't come anywhere near to God's
Let go, he says, and listen to me
For your heart is closed and your eyes tightly shut
So nothing can enter in

"I have so much to give you, my son,
If only you will listen to me
Put down your tools of the man my son
And pick up your heart instead

When you hold your heart in your loving hands
You will be living your life through me"
It is not easy this way, but the rewards will be great
And the better your Life will be
Listen closely my child to your loved ones and friends
For in them you will <u>hear my words</u>
That you need to move on and find your True Self
But the choice is always yours.

You can choose your old ways and sit in the dark
You can choose the way of the Light
The choice is yours, this is your second chance
Another world to experience and explore.

When the calls says "Wake up" you can go back to sleep

Or exist in the Love not the Fear
My word stays the same it is honest and true
For integrity is always the game.

The game is "Life" and the "Living" is good
When you Listen to those you love
Your name has been called and you've been told take your cue
From God who is TRUTH and LOVE.

You don't listen to this (Motor-heart) that drives you along
To this pump called the heart and what it is for
Your heart is closed and so cold to yourself
That you cannot let anyone in
So your heart hits back with a vengeance my child
To give you chance to STOP and listen within

The "connection" is clear, the connection is God
What else could the heart be for
It connects us all to the heart and mind of God
And he communicates through this organ,
<u>That is what it is for</u>.

And your feelings my friend are the way through to him
Your feelings are all in the heart
So next time you fall and pick yourself up
Listen carefully, he's talking to <u>you</u>.

Through your Anger and Pain through your Sadness and Guilt
He is trying to say just let go
Just <u>STOP</u>, <u>LOOK</u>, and <u>LISTEN</u> to what it's about
For you may not get another chance – it's UP TO YOU!

-o-o-0-o-o-

God's Commandments to ME

1. Live well – give yourself only the best
2. Eat well
3. Take good care of Yourself
4. Be Yourself
5. Don't listen to the Outside World, listen to me
6. Talk to me

I'm your FRIEND
I'm your Everything
I will meet all your Needs
I am your partner in life

7. Ask and Believe and it will be so
8. Trust totally in the Voice of your Heart (God) this is the most Selfless Act you can do, you will never be a burden to anyone on this Earth.
9. You don't need others to tell you how to take care of Yourself. You have <u>Intuition</u> "Inside tuition", so just listen within. When you can do all these you are ready to create your own world exactly as you desire it to be.

Co-creation with God.

-o-o-0-o-o-

FREEDOM AND JOY

Freedom is mine now I'm one with God
It's in loving and accepting my Self
And the "Self" is Spirit and God is LOVE
And his Creation is ME AS I AM.

My name's not important now I know who I am
The me that I was, has gone
All my questions are answered
No more searching to see

It's so clear now I'm focused on Oneness and Love

There is nothing missing
There is nothing lost
It's all there within me
THE ONE AND ONLY TRUE REALITY.

IT IS LOVE
I AM LOVE

THAT IS ALL THERE IS

GOD – EXPRESSED THROUGH ME AND THROUGH YOU AS ONE.

-o--o-0-o--o-

HOME AT LAST

My journey is complete and I am back where I belong
At home with God in my heart
I have opened the gates to the Kingdom within
And the Source of it all is revealed.

My life takes on new meaning
For it's all based on Love
No more Fear for me that's sure!
I rest in God's heart and the Peace and the Joy
Life is effortless, life is simple, life is ALL.

Nothing needed, nothing wanted
Now God has revealed
I have it all
I'm the Source of it all

I JUST THINK IT
                BELIEVE IT
                            AND SEE IT.

THERE ARE NO WORDS TO DESCRIBE THIS FEELING IN MY HEART
IT'S JUST A RADIANCE, A LIGHT SO BRIGHT – A LONE STAR WITH NOTHING TO DO BUT SHINE ...

-o-0-o-

TAKING CONTROL AGAIN

After total surrender, I have the reins again
And now I know how the journey works
No effort, no trying, just issue my command
And by God's grace it is done.
For my will and God's will are one and the same

No more separation, for that was the Pain
And the Aching to be ONE again
So the world moves around me and through me
And within me
But I always remain the same -I am not the BODY
I am Infinite spirit.

I am life and living
I am love

I am God, the Divine, the Buddha, the ALL
The stillness, the mystery, the wonder.

The WOW – WONDER OF WONDERS! CREATION. SO ARE WE ALL.

-o-o-0-o-o-

MY IDEA OF HEAVEN ON EARTH

Peace within when around me is Anger
Peace within when around me is Death
Contentment and Love are my only companions
In a world full of Fear and Distress

My thoughts are of Love and the Light of the World
My thoughts are of Colour and Joy
My thoughts are of helping my friends and companions
In getting and holding on tight to their world.

For my world inside me is beauty and Perfection
As God intended it to be
And when enough of us find it within our own hearts
Then Restored Our World will be to Wholeness.

-o-o-0-o-o-

DOORS WITHIN

Everyone and everything is a reflection of you. They all support the things you like and dislike about yourself.

The universe does not judge right and wrong, bad and good, it takes what you say and think about yourself very literally, so become aware of what you are thinking and saying.

- - - - -

OPENING THE DOORS WITHIN – INTO THE DEEPER MIND WHERE ALL YOUR THOUGHTS AND FEELINGS ARE STORED …

There are many, many ways but this is a really quick and simple technique to access your subconscious mind.

Sit quietly and take a few slow, deep breaths, close your eyes and visualise a corridor of many doors.

If this is difficult, first imagine your bedroom or where you live – you can either see, sense or feel it. It is different for everyone.

Some doors may have a feeling word such as Anger, Sadness, Pain or Fear. Some may have a number relating to a particular age. Some may have someone else's name on. See next page for some suggestions.

Ask which door do I need and take the word which comes into your mind. Notice if it appears locked or bolted. Use your imagination to unlock and look inside. It's the Wise you looking in so there is nothing to fear. Observe and ask any questions which come to mind, e.g. How do I feel in here? What do I need to change to make this into a peaceful or happy room (remember this is your heart space so make it really good).

This sends a message to your subconscious mind that your intention is to see it differently.

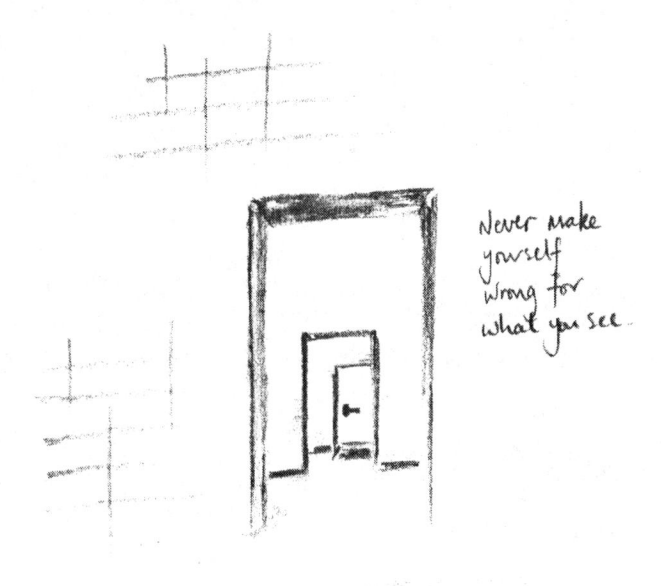

Never make yourself wrong for what you see

NEVER MAKE YOURSELF WRONG FOR WHAT YOU SEE.

If there's a door you don't want to deal with, acknowledge it and just leave it until another time when you feel able to look at it. YOU CAN ASK YOUR HIGHER MIND FOR COURAGE AND STRENGTH TO LEARN THE LESSON. When we just ask for something to be taken away without dealing with it, we are resisting what our Soul is teaching us.

SOME SUGGESTED DOORS TO TAKE YOU INTO YOUR DEEPER MIND…

SIT QUIETLY AND IMAGINE A CORRIDOR OF DOORS. WALK ALONG UNTIL YOU COME TO THE ONE YOU WANT, OR THE ONE THAT STANDS OUT. DON'T TRY TOO HARD. JUST LET IT HAPPEN. IT IS LIKE DAYDREAMING AND WE CAN ALL DO THAT, BUT THIS IS CONSCIOUS CREATING OF WHAT YOU WANT, RATHER THAN IMAGINING WHAT YOU DON'T WANT. WE DO THIS ALL THE TIME BASED ON DEEPER THOUGHTS AND FEELINGS FROM THE PAST. THIS JUST KEEPS US CREATING THE SAME SITUATIONS AND PROBLEMS AND LEAVES US FEELING INADEQUATE AND POWERLESS TO CHANGE OUR LIFE.

<u>HEAVY DOORS</u>

ANGER
HURT
PAIN
SADNESS
GUILT
RESENTMENT
JEALOUSY
HOLDING ON
FEAR
JUDGMENT
DENIAL
NOTHINGNESS
RESISTANCE
LIMITED
CONFUSED
PRESSURE

LIGHT DOORS
LOVE
PEACE
JOY
STILLNESS
BEAUTY
DIVINE
ABUNDANCE
GOD'S DOOR
LETTING GO
HEAVENLY
HOLY
PURITY
BLISS
HAPPINESS

DON'T SPEND A LOT OF TIME ON THIS – JUST LOOK INSIDE, SEE IT AS IT IS, ASK HOW YOU FEEL IN THERE AND WHAT NEEDS TO BE CHANGED. THEN USE YOUR IMAGINATION TO CHANGE THE ROOM TO WHAT YOU WANT – THIS STARTS THE DEEPER MIND KNOWING YOU WANT SOMETHING DIFFERENT.

FOR EXAMPLE, IF YOU GO INTO YOUR FEAR ROOM, IF IT IS DARK, PUT IN SOME LIGHT, CHANGE THE COLOUR. DO WHATEVER IS NECESSARY TO MAKE IT A SAFE SPACE, THEN BREATHE YOUR OWN LOVE AND LIGHT INTO THAT ROOM OR SPACE.

IF SOMEONE IS IN THAT ROOM, REMEMBER YOU HAVE THE POWER, TELL THEM WHAT YOU NEED TO, THEN REMOVE THEM FROM YOUR SPACE. AGAIN USE YOUR IMAGINATION. YOU DO NOT WANT OTHER PEOPLE IN YOUR HEADSPACE.

TRY CREATING YOUR PERFECT PEACE ROOM, OR INNER SACRED GARDEN, WHERE YOU CAN RELAX AND BE

STILL. BREATHE IN PEACE, HARMONY, LOVE AND BALANCE. IT TAKES PRACTICE BUT IT DOES WORK.

-x-x-x-x-x-

WHAT'S THE NEXT STEP NOW YOU SAY GOD, MY BOOK
IS COMPLETE.
JUST YOU WAIT AND I'LL TAKE CARE OF IT ALL
JUST LISTEN AND LEARN AND LEAVE IT WITH ME
AND MY MAGIC WILL ALL BE REVEALED.

AND THAT WILL BE MY NEXT BOOK ………
